Thanks!

Seeing God's World With A Grateful Heart

Seeing God's World With A Grateful Heart

A daily devotional on saying thanks

LESLIE B. FLYNN

 MAGNUS PRESS

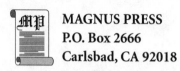

MAGNUS PRESS
P.O. Box 2666
Carlsbad, CA 92018

www.magnuspress.com

Thanks!: Seeing God's World with a Grateful Heart

Copyright © 2005 by Leslie B. Flynn

First Edition, 2005

Printed in the United States of America

LCCN: 2005931024
ISBN: 0-9724869-3-3

Publisher's Cataloging-in-Publication
(Prepared by The Donohue Group, Inc.)

Flynn, Leslie B.
    Thanks! : seeing God's world with a grate-
ful heart / by Leslie B. Flynn. — 1st ed.

       p. ; cm.
    ISBN: 0-9724869-3-3

1. Gratitude—Religious aspects—Christianity.
I. Title.
BV4647.G8 F59 2005
241/.4   2005931024

---

10 09 08 07 06 05   10 9 8 7 6 5 4 3 2 1

To

Peggy Brown and her late husband, Harry

and

Edison and Kay Bassett,

loyal friends for more than half a century
who have performed countless deeds of kindness and
for whom my wife, Bernice, our seven daughters, and I give
THANKS!

PREFACE

"Anything else to complain about, Les?" This question, gently asked by my good friend and college president as I chauffeured him to a dinner engagement, caught my attention. He was so right. On our way I had been grumbling about other drivers and stoplights and the slowness of service at the gas station. Is this the way I wanted to be remembered by my college president friend? It was time for me to reprogram myself to thankful thinking.

After all, doesn't godliness require the cultivation of a thankful disposition? Moses sang God's praises. David offered his Psalms. Daniel gave thanks three times a day. Jesus expressed appreciation to his heavenly Father on several occasions. Paul wrote of thanks at least 50 times, including six occasions in the short book of Colossians. And Paul commanded believers to be filled with the Spirit, listing inward melody and outward thanks as evidence of Spirit-filling. Godliness is impossible without gratitude.

A thankful heart has been termed not only the greatest virtue, but also the parent of all other virtues, the aristocrat of the emotions. Salvation, worship, generosity, contentment, morality, and dedication of life all involve thankfulness.

My wife, who was with me in the car that day, now smiles at me whenever I complain, and sweetly repeats my friend's question, "Anything else to complain about?" At that point I am reminded to swing into my thankful mode.

Studies tell us that daily gratitude exercises result in higher levels of enthusiasm, determination, optimism and energy. May the 366 musings in these pages help us enter God's gates with thanksgiving daily.

Leslie B. Flynn
Nanuet, New York

❧ January

❧ A Happier New Year

"Happy New Year!" How many times have you heard that greeting this season? People who genuinely use this expression are wishing good things to come your way: success at work, an enjoyable trip, good health, family well being, a growing stock portfolio.

One person who suffered a health crisis gives our popular New Year's greeting a deeper meaning. "Because of the stroke, I have received many of God's blessings. My daughters moved closer to help Mom and Dad, and my sons now visit when able to do so. I have plenty of time to meditate, to intercede. My spiritual life has blossomed and grown. When I get well, my theme will be: This is not just a material universe. The main dimension is spiritual. I wish you all a happier New Year, with our oneness in the Messiah—Christ our Lord."

It's not fame or fortune that brings a happier New Year, but a right relationship with God and man.

❧ A Refugee Revisits
January 2

In the late 70s, the West Linn Lutheran Church (in Oregon) sponsored Rathna Reth and 12 family members, refugees from Cambodia, providing a house, food, and jobs. The refugees became active members. After three years they moved to California where Reth worked in Silicon Valley.

In 2000 Reth and several family members visited their former church in West Linn. Although contacts were rare during the intervening years, Reth, now 34, wanted to present the congregation with a check for $10,000. Across the top he had written, "In gratitude to God for everything."

Those who knew the family said they always let the congregation know how thankful they were, but this was a special thoughtfulness.

Said one parishioner who had been his counselor in high school, "What is gratifying is not the money. It's the fact that he is successful and his spiritual life is in place—that's what's important."

❧ *January 3*   *If You Think, You'll Thank*

Dictionaries tell us that "thought" and "thank" are related. Someone does you a favor. In response you have a kind thought which prompts expression in word or deed. Thankfulness is rooted in thoughtfulness. In the old Anglo-Saxon, "think" and "thank" were substantially the same. Some scholars suggest that "thank" may be the past tense of "think," just as "drank" is the past tense of "drink." Gratitude has been defined as a "thankful sense of mercies received." Thinking should lead to thanking. "Think" and "thank" are twins.

In more than one language the word which means "favor" also means "thanks." The Latin "gratia" and the Greek "charis" both signify "favor," and "thanks for a favor," showing the bond between gift and gratitude.

Right thinking leads to grateful thanking. "Consider what great things he [God] has done for you" (1 Sam. 12:24).

❧ *January 4*   *Presbyterian Shoes*

In 1994 Pamela Baker Powell became the white pastor of a small black Presbyterian church in Lubbock, Texas. To combat drugs, with elder approval for a mission directed at the nearby elementary school, she offered three pupils in each class a pair of the finest athletic shoes for excellence in scholastics, citizenship or athletics. With 17 classrooms, cost was $10,000. Money came in. At semester end, honors were announced in a school assembly. Powell said, "When you go into Foot Locker, pick out any pair of shoes you want, because you have won." Some kids scoffed, "You'll just get some junky shoes."

That afternoon 40 of the 51 winners went to the mall to get their shoes. The Foot Locker manager said every child asked the same question, "Can I get anything I want?" He echoed Powell's line, "Yes, because you're a winner."

Next day in school, the principal said her office was overrun with grateful kids who wanted to show off their wonderful new shoes. AP picked up the story, dubbed "Presbyterian shoes."

⇛ Forget Not   *January 5*

A magazine publisher asked celebrities nationwide what they really wanted most. One famous architect wished for a garden and a small greenhouse. A noted writer said, "Give me my health and I'll be content." Another requested a little Vermont farm with a brook, apple orchard, and an old house furnished with antiques. A prominent lawyer desired one uninterrupted day at his home in the country with his grandchildren. But one of the most respected celebrities replied, "I would ask to be given an even greater ability to appreciate all that I now have."

The hymnwriter urges us to "Count your blessings, name them one by one." One songleader had the congregation sing, "Weigh them ton by ton." The Psalmist urges, "Forget not all his benefits" (103:2). We need to count—and recount.

⇛ Winning on TV   *January 6*

A few years ago on ABC's popular *Who Wants to Be a Millionaire*, one contestant, Dr. Mike Menz, an orthopedic surgeon who won $500,000, and member of a Lutheran Church in

Thanks!

Greeneville, Tennessee, told his fellow members, "The most spiritual moment of my life was on that show."

On this program the questions got harder as the prize money increased. Menz did well until he reached the $500,000 question. He had no idea of the right answer. Rather than panic, he recalls, "I just had this feeling that I was in God's hands and that it would be OK to take a chance." His answer was correct. Rather than risking the loss of most of his prize, he walked off with his $500,000.

Back in Greeneville, Menz tithed his prize money, donating $50,000 to his church. Menz, thankful to the Lord, said, "The experience gave me chills." His pastor was also grateful with a new 25-passenger minibus.

January 7   *The Lord's Mercies*

Jeremiah's "Lamentations" bemoan the terrible fate which befell Jerusalem when captured by the Chaldeans around 585 B.C. Planted right in the middle of the five chapters of dirges is an affirmation of God's goodness. "It is of the Lord's mercies that we are not consumed, because his compassions fail not. They are new every morning: great is thy faithfulness" (3:22-23, KJV). Someone punned, "In the midst of LAMENtations is an AMENtation."

The Lord's mercies are many. The Lord's mercies are varied. The Lord's mercies are new every morning. The Lord's mercies are of divine origin—His compassion and faithfulness. Often people are thankful for gifts, but fail to recognize the divine benefactor. How illogical to give more attention to the gift than to the giver and fail to trace the Lord's mercies back to the Giver.

January 8   *The Difference a Century Makes*

A recent documentary on Public Television depicted the reality of everyday living a century ago. In "The 1900 House," the camera follows the adventures of the Bowler family of six, living in a restored Victorian-era house in Greenwich, England.

It all seemed so exciting at first. Then the family discovered the downside of 1900 living: no phones, no computers, no TV, squeezing into a whalebone corset, keeping the cooking range stoked with coal, no electricity, no refrigeration, clouds of smoke and grime, unending labor, maddening boredom, and outside toilets. Very grueling was washday, an all-day affair including pounding and rubbing on a washboard. The children had their share of difficult home chores. Mostly they played fair, though once they sneaked a purchase of modern shampoo.

Viewer reaction—thanks for the difference 100 years make!

≫ Sunrise Faith   January 9

Paul uses the words "thanks," "thanksgiving," and "thankfulness" nearly 50 times, more than twice the number of times it is found in the rest of the New Testament. The concept of gratitude, important to Paul, should be so to us.

One thing we can be thankful for is sunrise. The sun comes up every morning and has for centuries, even though often obscured by clouds. After the Flood, God promised Noah he would never again destroy all living creatures. He said, "As long as the earth endures, seedtime and harvest, summer and winter, day and night will never cease" (Gen. 8:22). Day will always follow night.

So, the next time you find yourself in the middle of a bad situation, enclosed in darkness, a raging storm around, remember that no matter what, the sun will rise again. Be thankful that things will get better. This is "sunrise faith."

≫ Saturday Evening Post Cover   January 10

An exhibition of Norman Rockwell's Pictures for the American People drew big crowds at a Washington exhibit in 2000. On exhibit were all 322 covers he did for the *Saturday Evening Post* from the 1920s through the 1950s, including his famous "Rosie the Riveter."

In 1955 the *Saturday Evening Post* asked its readers to pick their favorite Rockwell cover. "Saying Grace" (1951) was the winner. This painting depicts a gray day with chilling winter rain. The scene is a working-class cafeteria by the rail yards. The place is crowded and dirty. A matron and her grandson have just taken two spare seats at a table near the window. About to taste their soup, they first bow their heads in prayer. A working guy at the same table with a union button on his cloth cap does not say grace in restaurants. Neither do most people today. But some still do bow their heads to say thanks.

⁂ *January 11*   A 9/11 Episode

During his State of the Union address in January 2002, President George W. Bush publicly spotlighted Lisa Beamer, whose husband, along with the heroic efforts of other passengers on a United Airlines plane over Pennsylvania, tried to overthrow their hijackers. Though they did not save the plane, experts agreed that they foiled the plan of the terrorists to damage a fourth target, perhaps the White House or Capitol Building. Lisa Beamer graciously acknowledged the standing ovation given her husband.

Todd had originally tried to reach his wife from the plane's onboard telephone, but his call was intercepted by the operator with whom he exchanged crucial information for the next 13 minutes. Todd learned from the operator about the three targets already hit, and she knew from his final words, "Let's roll," that he was giving a charge to his fellow passengers.

We will ever be thankful for the bravery and determination of Todd Beamer and his compatriots.

⁂ *January 12*   Calamity

According to *The Oxford Dictionary of Word Histories*, some Latin writers associated the word "calamity" with "calamus" (straw, corn stalk), referring to the damage to crops by drought, hail, insects or mildew. By medieval times the English word "calamity" came to mean any type of catastrophe. How calamitous life would be if we had no food.

Our generation is no stranger to famine. Literally millions have perished from starvation since the end of World War II. The media is continually displaying stark pictures of famished children, bones protruding from emaciated frames, eyes glazed. The tragedy of gnawing hunger vividly and repeatedly invades our homes.

Thanks, God, for giving us "our daily bread" (Matt. 6:11). And help us do our part to feed the hungry.

≫ A Forest Becomes a Sanctuary   *January 13*

Gilbert Beers, former editor of *Christianity Today*, traces his ancestry back to Catherine Dubois—his grandmother to the eighth great—of colonial times. In 1663 a raiding party of Indians attacked the village of New Palz, New York, killed several pioneers, and took Catherine and her infant daughter captive into the Catskill Mountains.

After ten weeks, the Indians roped Catherine and Sarah to a pile of logs and lit a torch. Moments away from a horrible doom, Catherine broke into a Huguenot hymn from her childhood, a song about the captivity of the Israelites in a strange land. Fascinated by Catherine's singing, the Indians demanded that she sing again and again. The dark forest became a sanctuary of thanksgiving as a choir of one sang praises to her God.

Says Beers, "A search party arrived and rescued Catherine, Sarah, and the next 10 generations, including me and my grandchildren." The songs of a thankful heart saved two lives and changed the course of history.

≫ Invitation to Worship   *January 14*

The greatness of God expressed in creation, providence, and redemption was a recurring reason for thanksgiving in the book of Psalms. David, thought to be the author of Psalm 95, wrote these lovely words that sound like tolling bells inviting the faithful to worship: "Let us come before him with thanksgiving and extol him with music and song. For the Lord is the great God, the great King above all gods. In his hand are the depths of the earth, and the mountain peaks belong to him. The sea is his, for he made it, and his hands formed the dry land. Come, let us bow down in worship ..." (vs. 2-6).

Attributes of God such as His omniscience, omnipresence, and omnipotence, truth, faithfulness, justice, righteousness, and love cause our thankful worship to spring forth. We join the songwriter in saying, "How great Thou art!"

⟫ *January 15*   *Majesty*

Both words and lyrics to one of our best-loved worship songs, "Majesty," were penned by California pastor Jack Hayford. Inspiration for this composition came to him when he and his wife were on a vacation traveling through Great Britain in 1977.

The itinerary included Blenheim Palace, an extensive estate built in the early 1700's for John Churchill, the first duke of Marlborough, and the birthplace of Winston Churchill two centuries later. Surrounded by this splendor, Hayford said to his wife, "there is majesty in all this." MAJESTY. The word lingered in his mind. With a thankful heart elevated to a higher majesty, he wrote a song to inspire believers to exalt the name of Jesus. It ends: "So exalt, lift up on high the name of Jesus, Majesty, worship His majesty, Jesus, who died, now glorified, King of all kings."

⟫ *January 16*   *From a Full Heart*

"Thanksgiving" consists of two words: "thanks" and "giving." We may give without thanking, but we cannot thank without eventually giving. Says the Psalmist, "Ascribe to the Lord the glory due his name; bring an offering and come into his courts" (Ps. 96:8).

There are two kinds of giving, forced and free. Forced giving says, "I have to give. It's my duty." Free giving says, "I want to give. I'm so thankful." The first has no song; the second flows from a full heart.

To secure the materials necessary for the construction of the tabernacle, Moses asked the Israelites, whose hearts were stirred and willing, to bring an offering. Gratitude motivated them to great giving, more than enough (Ex. 25:2; 35:21, 29; 36:7).

Thanks is the master key that opens purse and pocket.

⪼ The Happy Hour   January 17

When a preacher announces the offering, people don't usually shout "Amen!" Rather, a funeral atmosphere often prevails. Mendelssohn's "Consolation" would seem appropriate offertory music to make the extraction less painful as members of the congregation say a sad farewell to their money.

However, Paul has something to say about the frame of mind in which we give. He commands us "to give, not reluctantly or under compulsion" [not out of grief nor pressure], then adds, "for God loves a cheerful giver" (2 Cor. 9:7). The Greek word "cheerful" gives us our English "hilarious." Offering time should be a happy occasion. To think of what God has done for us in Christ, and to realize that God, who owns all, has given us the opportunity of giving to Him, should make us give an enthusiastic "Amen!" when the offering is announced.

⪼ Reminders   January 18

Thinking of God's many favors is a key to godly living. Contemplation leads to gratitude, which in turn motivates to dedication of life. The converse is likewise true. Thoughtlessness leads to thanklessness, which leads to transgression.

Man's memory is short and needs constant jogging. God gave the Israelites many reminders of His goodness, among them three national feasts designed to provoke gratitude (Ex. 23:14-17).

Thanks!

The Feast of Unleavened Bread reminded them of God's deliverance from Egyptian bondage. The Feast of Harvest (Pentecost) was a celebration of the first crops, and the Feast of Ingathering, when the harvest was completed in the fall, recalled God's faithfulness.

The Lord's Supper was also given as a memorial. Jesus said, "Do this in remembrance of me" (Luke 22:19). Meditation on the crucified body and shed blood of Christ should inspire us to renewal of our holy vows.

⋙ *January 19*   *Not Proud, but Grateful*

Parents are inclined to brag about their children and their exploits. That's what causes soccer madness—parents who berate coaches, demanding more playing time for their children.

When our children do excel in sports, school, music or some other area, parents should not brag, but display modesty. In his book, *Rebel With A Cause*, Franklin Graham tells the story of his years of waywardness, and of the overcoming of his rebellion through the grace of God. Today he serves as president of the Billy Graham Evangelistic Association and of Samaritan's Purse. As an evangelist he preaches to thousands of people in large stadiums.

When folks say to his parents, "You must be proud of Franklin," Billy and Ruth Graham respond, "We realize it is not a matter of pride, but of gratitude to God for His faithfulness."

⋙ *January 20* **Pastoral Prayer by Martin Luther King, Jr. (1956)**

"O God, our Heavenly Father, we come to thee today, grateful that thou has kept us through the long night of the past and ushered us into the challenge of the present and the bright hope of the future.

"We are mindful, O God, that man cannot save himself. Bound by sins, we know we need a Savior. Help us never to let anybody pull us so low as to cause us to hate. Give us strength to love our enemies and to do good to those who despitefully use us and persecute us.

"We thank thee for thy Church, founded upon thy Word, that challenges us to do more than sing and pray, but go out and work.

"Help us to walk together, pray together, sing together, and live together until that day when all God's children, Black, White, Red and Yellow will rejoice in one common band of humanity in the kingdom of our Lord and our God, we pray, Amen."

⇨ *Robbed!*　　　　　　　　　　　　*January 21*

Matthew Henry, author of an excellent commentary on the book of Matthew, was once accosted by robbers. Meditating on his experience, he penned these words in his diary: "Let me be thankful, first, because I was never robbed before; second, because they did not take my life; third, because, although they took my all it was not much; and fourth, because it was I who was robbed, not I who robbed."

The attitude of thanks in troublous times forces us to focus attention on our blessings, strengthens our faith in divine providence, fosters a happy, healthy outlook on life, is a potent witness to unbelievers, and shows obedience to the command to "Give thanks in all circumstances, for this is God's will for you in Christ Jesus" (1 Thess. 5:18).

⇨ *Some Day We'll Know*　　　　　　　*January 22*

Sometimes justification for our thankful attitude in the hour of disappointment becomes evident in a short time, perhaps even the same day. A young sailor, anxious to fly home, was bumped from his plane. Arriving home on another plane a few hours late, he learned that the first plane had crashed in the Rockies.

Sometimes it takes only a few days to see the silver lining. A college student broke his kneecap playing football. In the quiet of the hospital night hours he received a divine call to the ministry.

Thanks!

Or years may elapse before we see the reason. A wealthy but godless man was stricken with polio. A few years later he turned to the Lord. From his wheelchair he would praise Christ, "I thank you for my dear paralysis. Otherwise I might never have known you."

For those unanswered here on earth, some day heaven will make it plain.

❧ *January 23*   *A Letter Never Written*

Paul wanted to go to Rome as a preacher but he arrived as a prisoner, chained to a Roman soldier. His incarceration was irksome for a man of great energy and plans. He faced trial before the infamous Nero. Dr. Ralph Keiper imagines a letter the apostle might have written to the church at Philippi:

"Dear Brethren: I want you to know that I am in trouble. I'm in protective custody and I feel that the Lord has abandoned me. I resent it, and as far as serving the Lord further, I have decided to forget it. Who has been more faithful than I? Or traveled more miles? Or started more churches? And I had plans to evangelize Spain. Since I'm giving up, you may as well send my support money to someone else. Paul."

Paul did not write such a letter. A thankful attitude won out. See tomorrow's meditation.

❧ *January 24*   *All Expenses Paid*

Paul, a prisoner at Rome in a tough situation, could have reacted sulkily. Instead he expressed gratitude. Based on Philippians 1:12-18, Dr. Ralph Keiper imagines a letter Paul could have written:

"Dear Brethren: Do you know that in all of my missionary labors this is the first time I haven't had to go on deputation to raise funds? Also, I do not need to be bothered with traveling, because the government is bringing the congregation to me. They think I am the prisoner. If they only knew! They chain the guards to me—a captive audience. And then they tell their fellow guards what I have told them. They are my missionaries. Souls are being saved in Caesar's household.

"So, dear Philippians, since the Roman government is looking after me, the support you generally send to me send to another missionary in greater need. Do not worry about me, but be thankful for this marvelous opportunity for me to preach the Gospel in Rome. Yours in Him, Paul."

⁂ Not the "Wright" Choice   January 25

In early 1999 the Rev. Dr. Charles Wright received word of his appointment as the 59th chaplain of the U.S. Congress. Wright had been through the selection process and notified of his appointment. He was thankful. To make it official, the House had to vote on it.

In the meantime some congressmen discovered that the Rev. Timothy O'Brien, the only Catholic nominee among the final three, had been turned down for the post. They felt the decision was one of religious bias. The press called it an act of anti-Catholicism.

Wright was naturally disappointed that it was not a "Wright" choice for chaplain of Congress. Waiting for the decision, he felt the Lord calling him to another position, that of peacemaker. On March 22, 2000, he offered his letter of withdrawal. He called for unity and a spirit of love. He said, "Let us be thankful that God is not an Independent, not a Democrat, and not a Republican. He is for all of us."

⁂ Souper Bowl   January 26

At Spring Valley Presbyterian Church in Columbia, South Carolina, Pastor Brad Smith prayed, "Lord, even as we enjoy the Super Bowl football game, help us be mindful of those without a bowl of soup to eat." Wanting to transform Super Bowl Sunday into a day of caring, he suggested his Senior High Youth contact other youth groups in their area, and on Super Bowl Sunday parishioners in each church contribute $1 in large soup bowls at sanctuary exits. Twenty-two churches raised $5700 in the first SOUPER Bowl of Caring in 1990. In 2000 the total reached $3.1 million from 11,200 congregations in every U.S. state, Canada, and Puerto Rico. Over $10 million has been raised since the effort began.

100% of every dollar goes directly to the charity of each church's choice. Overhead expenses are raised independently. The SOUPER Bowl of Caring is a thankful response to God's love to care for the needy.

January 27   *General Thanksgiving*

From *The Book of Common Prayer*:
Almighty God, Father of all mercies, we, thine unworthy servants, do give thee most humble and hearty thanks for all thy goodness and loving kindnesses to us, and to all men . . . We bless thee for our creation, preservation, and all the blessings of this life; but above all, for thine inestimable love in the redemption of the world by our Lord Jesus Christ; for the means of grace and for the hope of glory. And, we beseech thee, give us that due sense of all thy mercies, that our hearts may be unfeignedly thankful; and that we show forth thy praise, not only with our lips, but in our lives, by giving up ourselves to thy service, and by walking before thee in holiness and righteousness all our days; through Jesus Christ our Lord, to whom, with thee and the Holy Ghost, be all honour and glory, world without end. Amen.

January 28   *Response in Trouble*

Dr. C. Everett Koop, former U.S. Surgeon General, became a believing member of the Christian community at age 30. "I wandered into the Tenth Presbyterian Church in Philadelphia one morning after hospital rounds. Donald Gray Barnhouse was then pastor. I became convinced of the truth of the gospel." Koop's faith in God became the driving force in his life. "I knew I was to practice my Christianity through my surgery." Motivated by thankfulness, he became a renowned pediatric surgeon. "Everything I value or do I consider a gift of God."

Koop was forced to rely on his faith when his 20-year-old son was killed in a mountain climbing accident in New Hampshire's White Mountains. Thankful even in that experience, he wrote a small book, *Sometimes Mountains Move*. It received more response than his popular work, *Whatever Happened to the Human Race*, co-authored with Francis Schaeffer.

⇛ Thank-You Notes   *January 29*

One lady makes it a practice of writing short but sincere thank-you notes to prominent performers for inspiration acquired from them. She isn't an autograph hound, nor does she have any expectation of meeting these eminent folk. But both she and the recipients of these unexpected notes are enriched.

Often the busiest people make time to write thank-you notes. When a college president was hospitalized for an eye operation in a Boston hospital, an alumnus dropped him a card with a note. To the alumnus' amazement he received an immediate acknowledgment in the president's own handwriting, in large, laborious letters.

Soon after U.S. soldiers arrived in Afghanistan in 2001, a rural 6th grade class wrote letters of support, all expressing the thought "Thanks for defending our country against evil. The world is behind you!"

⇛ Gratitude to Christ   *January 30*

Well-known Bible teacher Dr. Donald Grey Barnhouse had a flat tire driving in Alabama to a church service. A stranger offered to help. When he asked about all the books in the trunk, Dr. Barnhouse told him he was their author. The man said, "My wife would be interested. She teaches Sunday school. But I'm not interested."

All the time the man's dog stuck close. Often the man stopped to pat the animal. He explained, "Once when corralling cattle, I was caught in quicksand. I was all alone. This dog came along. By holding on to it, I was able to regain solid ground. That dog saved my life. I'm devoted to it. He eats at my table and sleeps in our bed."

Dr. Barnhouse commented, "How strange! A dog has saved your life and you are devoted to it. Yet Jesus Christ has done more than the dog. You are in a worse plight than quicksand from which Christ came to save you. The dog did not die for you, but Christ did! Yet you thank the dog, but you're not thankful to Christ!"

Unless the time comes when we say, "Thank you, Lord, for dying to save my soul," ingratitude to the Friend of friends will lock heaven's door against us. Gratitude to Christ brings us heaven's glories.

≫ *January 31*　　　　　*For What Was Jesus Thankful?*

When here on earth the Lord Jesus gave thanks on numerous occasions. Just think—the one who created the world, flung the stars into space, and upholds the universe by the word of His power, was a thankful person. For what did Jesus give thanks?

For food. Before both the feeding of the five thousand and the four thousand, He gave thanks (Matt. 14:19; 15:36).

For the hiding of spiritual insight from the so-called wise, and the granting of illumination to the simple (Matt. 11:25).

For answered prayer by His heavenly Father (John 11:42).

If the strong Son of God—Creator, Sustainer, and Redeemer—bothered to say thanks, how much more should frail, faltering human beings?

We should be thankful, not only for Him, but with Him.

❧ *February*

❧ *Thankful for the Olympics*   *February 1*

In the 1996 Olympics Sheila Taormina swam the third leg of America's gold medal, winning the 4x200-meter freestyle relay. She thought she was through with Olympic competition, so retired from swimming and devoted much of her time to speaking engagements. Soon she wondered if she had stepped away from swimming too early and began getting back into shape. After vigorous training and many competitions, she won the triathlon event in the Olympic Trials in May 2000.

In the 2000 Olympics, Taormina competed in the women's triathlon. She finished sixth, somewhat surprising since ranked only 57th worldwide at the end of 1999. Had she won a medal, she would have been the first American athlete ever to win medals at two different sports at two separate Olympics. Taormina commented, "My treasure isn't another gold medal. Rather, I'm thankful for the many opportunities to share my faith."

❧ *Senator Lieberman*   *February 2*

Senator Joseph Lieberman's bid to become vice-president failed in Al Gore's loss in the fall 2000 election. But we did come to learn much about Lieberman. When he flew to Tennessee to stand by Gore's side and be announced as Gore's running-mate, the papers claimed that as he opened his remarks, Lieberman digressed from his prepared text, quoted Scriptures and thanked God for his good fortune.

He often talks about how the Talmud collection of Jewish law and tradition inspires him. A few years ago he and lawyer Bill Bennett handed out "Silver Sewer Awards" to single out producers of sexually explicit and violent films, music, TV programs and video games.

Lieberman observes the Jewish Sabbath. He says, "My faith is part of me. It's been the center of who I've been all my life. Without God, I wouldn't be here." Thankfulness is a part of his life.

≫ *February 3*   *A Vanishing Practice*

During the first year of the Pilgrims in the New World over half the colony perished from malnutrition and disease. But these Pilgrims were still thankful to God, and after a good harvest in 1621, Governor Bradford ordered a three-day worship at which they ate turkey.

Three hundred years later, a national magazine reported that only one person in sixty turned out for Thanksgiving services in Plymouth where Thanksgiving started.

So vanishing is the practice of saying grace that when someone does so in a restaurant, those at nearby tables may wonder if that person is strange or sick. After donating blood, a sophomore received his usual cup of juice and sandwich, then bowed his head. Nurses grabbed him before he could explain that he was just saying grace, not passing out.

We still eat turkey. Do we still thank God?

≫ *February 4*   *The Source of Wealth*

The destruction of the World Trade Towers on 9/11/2001 should remind us how fragile is our prosperous style of living.

The Lord warned Israel that when they reached the Promised Land and built fine homes and possessions multiplied, they should not proudly say to themselves, "'My power and the strength of my hands have produced this wealth for me.' But remember the Lord your God, for it is he who gives you the ability to produce wealth . . ." (Deut. 8:11-18).

How easy in our blessed America to conclude that all these things—our bank accounts, our stock portfolios, our lovely homes and furniture, our vacations, our high salaries and bonuses—we somehow earned by our own initiative, our own ingenuity, our own industry!

If only we would pause to ponder, we would remember to give God the credit, and thank Him by living a life of gratitude.

⁂ Baby "81"   *February 5*

The story of "Baby 81" was a rare bright spot in the catastrophic tsunami that killed over 200,000 people in South Asia on Dec. 26, 2004. He was found amid mud, debris, and corpses after the killer waves receded after battering Kalmunai, Sri Lanka. The baby was so named because he was the 81st admission to the hospital the day the tsunami hit.

Nine couples claimed the boy in the following days. No one could document the birth because all records were lost in the storm. One couple, the Jeyarajahs, who said their baby had been swept from his mother's arms, launched an agonizing court battle to claim him. So the court ordered DNA tests at a clinic in Sri Lanka's capital. Based on the tests, the court ruled that the baby belonged to the Jeyarajahs.

The joyous father exclaimed, "I am so happy, and I have only to thank God for giving my child back."

⁂ Spectacular Gift   *February 6*

Newsweek's cover once carried this striking statement, "Of all the singular gifts bestowed on human beings, the ability to speak is perhaps the most miraculous and the most taken for granted."

Only man has the physical apparatus to produce involved linguistic sounds. Inanimate nature does not speak. Dogs bark.

Thanks!

Cats meow. Sheep go baaah. Because humans can think discursively, God has given them highly developed voice boxes, which permit them to express what they are thinking. How thankful we should be for this gift, and how careful!

When Thomas Edison was honored at a banquet for his many inventions, especially the talking machine, he insisted on a correction. "It was God who invented the first talking machine. I only invented the first one that could be shut off!"

≫ *February 7*   ***Thankful Desperadoes***

An older guard, named Adams, known for his kindness to prisoners in a tight security section of Georgia St. Penitentiary, died of a fatal heart attack. Several inmates signed a letter to Adam's wife, saying, "Your husband was one of the finest men we have ever met." Next day Mrs. Adam asked the warden if these men could attend her husband's funeral. The warden pondered— 13 desperadoes, each with at least one life sentence! The inmates promised him they would not make any attempt to escape.

It was 20 miles from prison to church. Unarmed guards marched the inmates inside. The church filled. When the service ended, the widow walked to the prison bus. "We feel honored that all of you would come. Thank you for your behavior. My husband spoke highly of you." Riding back, one inmate said, "Imagine being out in the woods and not trying to escape. But I just can't run. Adams meant too much to me."

≫ *February 8*   ***The Faithfulness of God***

Promises are broken. Contracts are violated. Marital vows are dishonored. Pacts among nations become scraps of paper. But thank God for His faithfulness in both the world and in His Word.

In the World. Because God is faithful in His world, we can predict eclipses to the split second. The constancy of God in nature makes possible the discovery of the laws of science.

In the Word. The promises of God are "Yes" in Christ. He never falters, forgets, nor fails, for He is faithful to forgive confessed sin, to provide a way out of temptation, and to preserve us until the day of His coming (1 Jn. 1:9; 1 Cor. 10:13; I Thess. 5:23-24).

A dying man, with failing memory, said, "I can't remember a single promise, but that doesn't matter. God does not forget any."

⇛ The Gutenberg Press   *February 9*

The cable TV network, A&E, aired a series entitled "Biography of the Millennium: 100 People—1,000 years." They selected a list of the most influential people of the past millennium. Their selection of first place was Johann Gutenberg whose metal moveable-type printing press in the 15th century made it possible for information to be widely disseminated, and helped fuel cultural changes including the Reformation and the Enlightenment.

What drove Gutenberg was a mission to make the word of God available to everyone. Lamenting that religious truth was imprisoned in a small number of manuscript books, he said of his press, "Through it God will spread His word, causing a light heretofore unknown to shine amongst men."

The fruit of his labor was a three-volume, Latin version of the Holy Scriptures, completed in Mainz in 1455. About 200 copies of the Gutenberg Bible were printed. One resides in the Library of Congress.

Thank God for Gutenberg's contribution to the world.

⇛ Enough to Eat   *February 10*

During the depression in Chicago where I was a pastoral student, I was on my way to the Easter Sunrise Service in Soldiers Field. As my elevated train stopped at a station over a busy avenue, looking down, I saw a shabbily dressed vagrant tilting a garbage can, reaching in, scooping out discarded food, and

Thanks!

shoving it into his mouth.

Millions in our world go to bed hungry every night. In a poor hill tribe in Colombia, South America, a Christian national could not understand the meaning of the New Testament word "glutton." Even after explanation he could scarcely grasp its significance, simply because he rarely ever had enough to satisfy his hunger.

We often fail to give thanks for food by remembering where all food comes from. Were it not for the Lord God we would not eat.

⇒ *February 11*   *In the Presence of Enemies*

An estimated half a million believers lost their lives during the despotic regime of Idi Amin in Uganda. One day a busload of Christians was surrounded by security forces just before starting a trip to a Christian revival conference. A security official led them to a prison where they knew anything could happen under Amin's rule of terror.

Soon one of them started singing the familiar East African Revival song, Tukutendereza Yesu in a subdued tone:

"Tukutendereza Yesu"   (We praise you Jesus),
"Yesu Omwana gw'endiga" (Jesus lamb of God).

In no time the entire prison yard was resounding with song. Soldiers ran to watch, then brought them food. How thankful they were for the table prepared for them in the midst of their enemies (Ps. 23:5).

⇒ *February 12*   *The First Thanksgiving Day*

President Abraham Lincoln considered the Civil War a divine judgment on the nation. In proclaiming April 30th, 1863, a day of national humiliation, fasting, and prayer, he wrote, "We have forgotten the gracious hand which preserved us in peace, and multiplied and enriched and strengthened us. And have vainly imagined in the deceitfulness of our hearts that all these blessings were produced by some superior wisdom and virtue of our own. Intoxicated with unbroken success, we have become too self-sufficient to feel the necessity of redeeming and preserving grace, too proud to pray to the God that made us."

Later that year, on October 3rd, Lincoln proclaimed the first national annual Thanksgiving Day as now observed, inviting his fellow citizens "to set apart and observe the last Thursday of November next as a day of thanksgiving and praise to our beneficent Father."

⁂ Divine Protection   *February 13*

Camouflage, a military device, is also a strategy of the animal world, enabling them to hide from their enemies. Caterpillars, slow moving and for the most part non-poisonous and very vulnerable, are able to blend with the leaves on which they crawl, making themselves invisible to passing birds. The Caligo butterfly of South America has markings like the eyes of an owl which often frightens away birds that would otherwise eat it.

A deer can stay motionless and merge into its natural background. Even the opossum uses a form of camouflage, pretending death so successfully that "playing possum" has become part of our language.

Where did creatures of nature get their ability to camouflage and to do it so well? In His goodness God has made nature this way, another reason to thank God. The Psalmist wrote, "O Lord, you preserve both man and beast" (36:6).

⁂ Overcoming an Overwhelming Loss   *February 14*

Three days before the Sydney 2000 summer Olympics ended, Glory Alozie flew home to Nigeria. Also on the plane was a casket carrying the body of her fiancé, Hyginus Anayo Anugo. The night before flying home Glory had finished second in the 110-meter hurdles.

Thanks!

Hyginus, a member of the men's relay team, had arrived in Sydney ahead of Glory who had a meet in Japan. Before her arrival he was tragically killed by a car while crossing a street in a Sydney suburb. Overwhelmed by the news, she thought of not running in the Olympics and didn't eat for 12 days. Her coach had to spoon-feed her. With his encouragement and patience she came in second. They had met while competing in the same running club and were inseparable. Friends called them, "such giving Christians."

Maintaining a thankful stance, Glory said, "God saw me through this difficult time, and I know He'll see me through difficult times ahead."

※ *February 15*　　　　　　　　　　**"Trust Me," Saith the Lord**

Decades ago a Philadelphia pastor asked for testimonies in a prayer meeting of those who had tithed for several years. Six gave thankful witness to blessings received. The seventh, a frail woman of 70, said, "I wish I could bear such testimony but I cannot. I have skimped and denied myself through the years to keep a vow made many years ago to tithe, but now I am old and losing my position and have no means of support. I don't know what I shall do." The meeting closed in a chill.

Next day the pastor, Dr. Conwell, was lunching with his friend, John Wanamaker, founder of Wanamaker's department store, who remarked, "Our store is about to inaugurate a pension system for our employees. We issued our first life pension today to a woman who has served our firm for 25 years." It was she who had given the pessimistic testimony in prayer meeting the night before. What great thanks she gave to God upon hearing the news!

※ *February 16*　　　　　　　　**Splendor Through Common Grace**

In his book *Reaching for the Invisible God*, Philip Yancey says he "turned to God primarily because of my discovery of goodness and grace in the world: through nature, through classical music, through romantic love. Enjoying the gifts, I began to seek the giver; full of gratitude, I needed Someone to thank . . . God had been there all the while, waiting to be noticed."

To illustrate, Yancey tells of leaving a New Year's Eve party in Colorado just before midnight. Unaware of a New Year's Eve custom of mountaineers shooting off fireworks at the top of Pike's Peak, suddenly at midnight he saw red, blue, and yellow bits of light, forming huge, gorgeous flowers gliding slowly in the sky, illuminating Pike's Peak.

The mountain was there all the time but he needed light to see it. The light of God's common grace often leads to the majesty of His pardon.

⫸ Handwritten Thank-You Notes — *February 17*

Richard Nixon and John Kennedy had been bitter political enemies. When the official White House portraits of John and Jacqueline Kennedy were ready for unveiling in 1971, the Nixons were in the White House. Mrs. Kennedy was dreading the unveiling. To make it easier, President and Mrs. Nixon invited Jacqueline, Caroline, and John, Jr. for a private dinner—without press—just the Nixons and the Kennedys.

In the Nixon archives are two handwritten thank-you notes. One is from Jacqueline Kennedy. The other is from John, Jr., then ten:

"Dear Mr. President, Dear Mrs. Nixon, I don't think I remember much about the White House but it was really nice seeing it again . . . I loved the pictures of the Indians. The soufflé was the best I have ever tasted. I liked seeing the President's office a lot. Sincerely, John Kennedy."

⫸ Not Just Before Eating — *February 18*

In his essay "Grace Before Meat," Charles Lamb confessed that meditation on the many goodnesses of God made him want to say grace not just before eating, but for numerous reasons. "I own that I am disposed to say grace upon twenty other occasions in the course of the day besides my dinner." He added that he wanted a form of thanks for beginning a pleasant walk, for a moonlight ramble, for a friendly meeting, or a solved problem." He asked, "Why have we none for books—grace before Shakespeare?"

Paul told the Ephesians to always give "thanks to God the Father for everything"(5:20).

Every time we return from a trip we should thank God for safety. Every time the fire whistle blows, or the ambulance goes by, we should be grateful for protection and health.

≫ *February 19*   *On a Baby's Safe Arrival*

When Hannah, long childless, gave birth to baby Samuel, she offered a prayer of thanksgiving (1 Sam. 2:1-10), and brought him as a child to the Tabernacle to be reared by the high-priest Eli.

The English *Book of Common Prayer* contains a prayer called "The Thanksgiving of Women After Child-birth":

O Almighty God, we give thee humble thanks that thou has been graciously pleased to preserve, through the great pain and peril of child-birth, this woman; thy servant who desireth now to offer her praises and thanksgivings unto thee. Grant, we beseech thee, most merciful Father, that she, through thy help, may faithfully live according to thy will in this life, and also may be partaker of everlasting glory in the life to come; through Jesus Christ. Amen.

How wonderful when any mother, like Hannah, not only offers thanks for a safe delivery, but also gives her newborn back to the Lord.

≫ *February 20*   *God's Providence*

Over a century ago four Scottish ministers traveled in the Mideast to scout good localities for Jewish missionary work. In Egypt one minister suffered a bad fall from his camel and returned home. In Austria another preacher took sick with cholera. A Christian archduchess, learning the reason for their travels, promised support for any mission started among the Jews in her locality. This remarkable chain of events led to many conversions, among them Alfred Edersheim and Adolph Saphir, whose scholarly writings are found in many theological libraries today.

Joseph must have been bitter when his brothers sold him into slavery. But he learned to be grateful, later saying to his brothers, "You intended to harm me, but God intended it for good to accomplish . . . the saving of many lives" (Gen. 50:20). Ill is good if God is in it.

⇨ New Shoes   *February 21*

Mark Buchanan tells of attending a Sunday evening service a few years ago in Uganda, Africa. A lady came forward to testify, "Oh, how good Jesus is. I love Him so much. For three months I prayed for shoes. And look"! She pointed to her shoes; the crowd clapped and shouted. Buchanan said, "In all my life I had not once prayed for shoes. And in all my life I had not once thanked God for the many, many shoes I had. As I later tried to sort that out, I looked at a lot of Scriptures about being thankful. I discovered that being thankful and experiencing the power and presence of Jesus Christ are tightly entwined. I read 1 Thess. 5:18: 'No matter what happens, always be thankful.'"

Buchanan summed it up. "To know God is to thank God. To worship God is to thank God. And to thank God in all things and for all things is to acknowledge that God is good, just, and powerful."

⇨ Spectacular or Simple   *February 22*

The apostle Paul was thankful for his transformed life. Before his conversion he had led the attack on the early church and assisted in the death of Stephen. A few years later he wrote, "I thank Christ Jesus our Lord, who has given me strength, that he considered me faithful, appointing me to his service. Even though I was once a blasphemer and a persecutor and a violent man, I was shown mercy" (1 Tim. 1:12-13). The chief of sinners had become the apostle to the Gentiles.

Even though our conversion may not have been as spectacular as Paul's, we should give thanks, perhaps even greater thanks. In a testimonial meeting led by the early 20th-century evangelist Gypsy Smith, man after man arose to tell of his sordid past: prison, alcoholism, counterfeiting, and thievery. Smith commented, "God did more for this gypsy boy than for all of you put together. He saved me before I got where you did!"

February 23   *The Basic Motivation*

The Tenth Commandment, "You shall not covet," may seem inconsequential because it does not deal with some serious act but merely prohibits a sin of the thought life. Yet covetousness is the egg which hatches into major outward iniquities like stealing, slander, adultery, even murder. Covetousness can be overturned by thankfulness. Reformed theologians considered the Ten Commandments not as a way to earn heaven, but as definite ways believers should express their gratitude to God. Because God has been merciful through Christ we should love God and our neighbor. Loving gratitude toward a neighbor leads to concern for his property, reputation, marriage, and life.

James I. Packer, noted theologian, says, "From the plan of salvation I learn that the true driving force in authentic Christian living is not the hope of gain, but the heart of gratitude."

February 24   *Compassion for God's Children*

A reporter, covering the war in Sarajevo, saw a little girl shot in the head by a sniper. The reporter helped the little girl and the man holding her into the reporter's car. As they raced to the hospital, the man holding the bleeding child said, "Hurry, my friend, my child is still alive!" A moment later, "Hurry, my friend, my child is still breathing." Finally, "Hurry, oh my friend, my child is getting cold."

When they reached the hospital, the little girl had died. As the two men stood in the washroom, wiping the blood off their hands, the man turned to the reporter and said, "I have a terrible task to do. I must tell her father that his child is dead. He will be heartbroken."

The reporter was astounded. "I thought she was your child."

The man replied, "No, but aren't they all our children?"

Thank God for all who show compassion for suffering children.

⇒⇒ Jesus Paid Our Debts   *February 25*

A Russian Czar used to enjoy mingling with his subjects incognito. One night while visiting the soldiers' barracks, he spotted a young officer in his tent sitting at a table with his head on his arm, sound asleep. On the table he saw a loaded revolver and a paper on which was a long list of gambling debts, and written below, "Who can pay so much?"

In a flash the Czar grasped the situation. The young officer had gambled all he had and intended to blow his brains out. The Czar decided to report him. Then he remembered that the boy's father was his friend. So, underneath "Who can pay so much?" he wrote "Alexander."

The youth awoke, took his revolver, then suddenly noticed another word on the paper, "Alexander." In amazement he dropped his gun. He recognized the handwriting. It was the Czar's. Next day a messenger came with a bag of money from the Czar. His life was saved.

We are in enormous debt to God. Who can pay the penalty for our sins? Jesus came to earth and "paid it all." Thank you, Jesus.

⇒⇒ Did I Say Thanks?   *February 26*

A lady sent a wedding gift to a bride. She received no acknowledgment. A church sent packages to two dozen students away at college. Only three sent thank-you notes. At Thanksgiving, an employer sent 175 choice turkeys to each of his employees. Only four thanked their employer.

In the days of the judges, Gideon rescued Israel from its enemies and ushered in 40 years of peace. After his death Israel
reverted to idol worship. Not only did they forget the Lord, but
"They also failed to show gratitude to the family of . . . Gideon for
all the good things he had done for them" (Judg. 8:35). No thanks.

A newspaper columnist reported that of all the kids who
paraded to her door on Halloween, only a third of them thanked
her when she put candy in their bags. The rest just turned and
walked away. She could only mutter to herself, "Won't you please
say 'thank you'"!

⟫ *February 27*   **Smart and Not So Smart**

Thanks was given by Jesus to His heavenly Father because He
had revealed spiritual truth to the untutored while hiding such
matters from the intelligentsia. Jesus prayed, " I thank thee, O
Father . . . because thou hast hid these things from the wise and
prudent, and hast revealed them unto babes" (Matt. 11:25, KJV).

The untutored can apprehend saving truth. Lack of education does not disqualify. Those who realize their emptiness
receive divine wisdom more readily than those smugly filled with
their own learning. Know-it-alls have little room for more
knowledge. The proud Pharisees did not believe Jesus' deity, but
this basic truth was revealed to simple Peter.

After the resurrection Jesus did not appear to unbelievers like
Pilate, Annas, Caiaphas, or Sadducees or Pharisees. But he did
show himself alive to his disciples repeatedly. Thank God for
simple, childlike faith.

⟫ *February 28*   **Wires Crossed**

The pastor of a church called Almighty God Tabernacle,
working late one Saturday night, called his wife to let her know he
wouldn't be home for a while. The phone rang several times

unanswered. He thought it strange and decided to try later. When he called her the second time, she answered immediately. He asked why she didn't answer before. She said the phone hadn't rung. They forgot about it.

On Monday the pastor received a call at the church. The caller wanted to know why the pastor had called him Saturday night. "My phone rang," the voice said, "but I didn't answer. I was terribly depressed and about to commit suicide, and I prayed, 'God, if you exist and you don't want me to do this, give me a sign now.' At that point my phone started to ring. I looked at the caller ID and it said 'Almighty God.' I was afraid to answer."

The pastor told of his unanswered call on Saturday evening. Though neither could explain how the mix-up occurred, both thanked God for making the wrong number turn out to be the right number.

ᐁ *Savior and Example*   *February 29*

Christ is not only our Savior, but He is also our model. After washing His disciples' feet Jesus said, "I have set you an example that you should do as I have done for you" (Jn. 13:15).

The Church has not always maintained balance between the two truths—that He is both Savior and example. Those who omit salvation through the cross nullify the gospel, while those who neglect the believer's responsibility to follow the model of Christ downgrade the Christian life. We need to emphasize both faith in Christ, and conformity to His character.

Oswald Chambers' words in the rotunda of the Billy Graham Center: "If Jesus were only a Teacher, all He can do is to tantalize us by erecting a standard we cannot come anywhere near. But if we know Him first as Savior by being born again from above, we know that He did not come to teach us only: He came to make us what He teaches we should be."

We should be thankful He's *both* Savior and Example.

March

Ranald, a 14th century European king, glaringly overweight, was overthrown by his younger brother, Edward. Edward removed Ranald from the throne and built a special dungeon with no door but a door-sized opening. However, Ranald was too corpulent to get out. Edward said, "When you can fit through the doorway, you can leave." Inside the room Edward placed all the essentials Ranald would need. Every day Edward's servants brought a huge supply of pastries, pies, and platters of meat and other delicacies.

Ranald remained in that same room for more than ten years, till Edward was killed in battle. It was not because Ranald had no choice, but because he was a slave to his own appetite. He could not resist temptation.

We are all tempted. But thank God that when temptation does come He has promised to always provide a doorway out (1 Cor. 10:13).

Marla Runyan is the first athlete to make the jump from the Paralympics for the disabled to the regular Olympics. In 1996 she was a multi-event winner in the Atlanta Paralympics. In 2000 she qualified to represent the USA at the Sydney Olympics.

She suffers from Stargardt's Disease and is legally blind. Marla can't make out the faces of people. The track is about all she can see. If leading in a race, she may have no idea what's going on around her.

At the Sydney games she qualified for the 1500-meter final and led part way, eventually finishing 8th. Runyan has been a source of great inspiration to all disabled.

She's thankful because, "I know I can impact on other lives in a positive way. My race only takes four minutes, but the difference I can make for other people will last a lot longer."

≫ The Place Where Thanks Was Given   *March 3*

Big Brother, a 2000 CBS TV series, isolated 10 strangers to live three months in the same house under constant scrutiny of several microphones and cameras, which made public their every word and move. When they sat down to their first meal, someone asked, "Are we going to say grace?" The group dismissed the matter as a triviality.

Some Christians today are ashamed to bow their heads in a restaurant, even to silently thank God for their food. Yet the Lord Jesus bowed His head in a crowd of 5,000 men, women and children, and audibly voiced His thanks (Matt. 14:19).

The disciples connected Jesus' grace with the feeding of the 5,000. Writing his Gospel story more than half a century later, John identified a place on the Sea of Galilee "where the people had eaten the bread after the Lord had given thanks" (6:23.) The giving of thanks loomed as memorable as the miracle of the loaves and fishes.

≫ Giving God the Praise   *March 4*

So often we forget to thank God when He has reached down and extricated us from some seemingly impossible dilemma. In our predicament we may have made some strong promise to the Lord.

A young man in his mid-twenties, seriously injured in an accident, hovered between life and death for three months. The boy had stopped attending church a year before the accident. His pastor stopped by the hospital every few days. One day he heard the boy mutter, "I'll—be—in church every Sunday." Accustomed to hearing such promises, the pastor gave it little thought. To his amazement a few months later the boy, partially recovered, shuffled into church and attended regularly thereafter.

That first morning he said to the pastor, "I'm thankful to God for letting me have the strength to come." The boy did not forget to praise God.

☞ *March 5*   **Behind a Thank-You**

The pastor of an Anglican church in Brazil answered a knock at his door. A stranger wanted money to buy medicine for his sick child. The cautious pastor asked for the prescription and told the stranger to return in an hour. He bought the medicine and was waiting for the stranger, who thanked the pastor profusely. The pastor said, "I want to go with you." He knew the man could sell the medicine and buy alcohol.

They drove in the pastor's car several miles to a village of about 50 families, poor, mixed, despised, with many children, no employment, no water, no electricity, no sanitation. As a result, the pastor returned many times to that village. He taught them to bake bread, to plant a garden, to petition city hall, to found a school.

Recently the pastor received nearly forty of their adults into his church, and they've got a church school going. All this because he went beyond the first thank-you, and found a much deeper need.

☞ *March 6*   **God's Minor Mercies**

Through English history some special events caused the proclamation of a Day of Thanksgiving: like the defeat of the Spanish Armada in 1588, the 60th year of the reign of Queen Victoria in 1897, and the end of World War I in 1918 and World War II in 1945.

Does human nature tend to express gratitude for major miracles and take for granted minor mercies? If some distant uncle left us a fortune, we would rejoice. But how about the common ways in which the Lord bestows His goodness on us?

Observant Jews, on awakening, say thanks for the day, for the power of sight, for the creation of the earth, for the power to walk, for the renewal of strength, for not being an idolater or a slave. They also offer special thanks for the sight of trees in the springtime, the ocean, a rainbow, and new possessions.

⫸ *Cow, Grasshoppers, Books, and Manual*　　*March 7*

Susan Hay, veteran missionary in the Republic of Congo, has seen the devastation of the war there as well as the genocide in neighboring Rwanda. Despite the difficulties, she recently cited a few of the myriad ways in which God has recently manifested his favor:

A cow: Cows are perhaps the most important "currency" in this region of Africa. No greater present can one offer. She was given one.

Mushenenes: Large grasshoppers that come just once a year, which when fried and salted, are considered delicacies. She was given a bagful.

Good books that God brings into her life just at the right moment.

AIDS manual: She is thankful for divine help in writing a comprehensive AIDS manual targeting Rwandan church teenagers.

She ends, "Pray that midst all the grief I will recognize his daily blessings and that I will live in a spirit of thanksgiving."

⫸ *Light Therapy*　　*March 8*

Recent studies have shown that the short days of winter can bring on serious depressions, clinically termed "Seasonal

Affective Disorder" (or SAD). SAD is different from the Holiday Blues that come at Christmas or New Year's. Rather, SAD occurs regularly with the onset of fall and winter's short days, and leaves in the spring.

Recent research has discovered that two or three hours of very bright light, soon after the patient arises, is effective. Many patients start getting relief in just a few days of "light therapy". If you live in the North, a mid-winter vacation in a southern climate is suggested.

How symbolic that the winter solstice, the peak of the dark days, is immediately followed by the celebration of the birth of Jesus, whom John calls the True Light (1:5-9). Thanks for Jesus Christ, the Light of the world, who came into the world to dispel our gloom and darkness.

≫ *March 9*   *So Many Bibles*

At one time churches in England had one large copy of the English Bible chained up at the front. Today—so many Bibles!

Some titles: The Spirit-Filled Life Bible, Charles Haddon Spurgeon's Devotional Bible, Life Application Bible, Good News Bible, Scofield Reference Bible, Bible in Cockney, The King James Extra-Large Print Bible, Women's Devotional Bible, Marriage Devotional Bible, Quick Reference Bible, Smallest Bible, Illustrated Family Tree Bible, NIV Thin-Line Bible, Young Explorer's Bible, Ryrie Study Bible, Passages of Life Bible, New King James Mother's Love Bible, Teen Study Bible, One-Minute Bible, New Living Translation Bible, Exhaustive Thompson Topical Bible, New Oxford Annotated Bible, The Bible in Pictures for Little Eyes, Serendipity Bible, King James Comfort Print Bible, International Inductive Study Bible, Life Application Red Letter Study Bible, and more.

Indeed, we are grateful for the availability of so many versions, and for publishers who make such wide access possible.

❧ *His Eye Is on the Sparrow* *March 10*

A news report from London, England reads, "One train was canceled and three were delayed because of a swan with a broken leg. The swan could not move off the tracks near Waterloo station. The engineer of the first train waited till the bird could be safely removed."

In Florida a new road was under construction, and trees had to be cut down. The superintendent noted that one tree had a nest of birds not yet ready to fly. He ordered that the tree be left standing to be cut down later. A few weeks later the superintendent came back to an empty tree. The tree was felled. The nest fell out, scattering bits of paper. One piece fluttered near the feet of the superintendent. He picked it up. It had been torn from a Sunday school paper—on it these words, "He cares for you" (1 Pet. 5:7).

We can be thankful that the Father's eye is on the sparrow, and that He also watches us.

❧ *Kindness to Creatures* *March 11*

A visitor to South America one day heard the cries of a bird which kept fluttering over her nest on a lower branch of a nearby tree. The visitor soon grasped the situation. Creeping slowly toward the tree was a poisonous snake with its eye fixed on that nest of little ones and frightened mother. Strangely, the male bird, hovering nearby, flew away and soon returned, carrying a twig in its mouth. Laying the twig across the nest, he fluttered to a higher branch to watch. By this time the snake had reached the tree. Gliding along the branch, it came close to the nest, lifted its venomous head, then suddenly throwing its head back, it turned, climbed down, and disappeared.

The visitor later learned that the twig brought by the male bird and placed on the nest is poisonous to that kind of predator snake. The little helpless bird had used the twig as a shield of defense. For God's protective kindness to his creatures we bow in wonder and thanks.

A little girl fumbled around so noisily in her purse at offering time that her mother asked, "What are you looking for?"

The girl replied, "I'm looking for another quarter. If God is as good as the minister says, then I'm raising His allowance."

Tithing, a difficult practice for many moderns, can be made more palatable if hearts are first made thankful. Had the Israelites of Malachi's day felt genuine gratitude to God they would never have withheld the tithe, nor offered blind, lame, and sick animals as sacrifices (Mal. 1:6-9).

With keen insight gained from learning at Jesus' feet, Mary expressed her thanks to Jesus for his imminent sacrifice by anointing him in advance of his burial. The spices equaled a year's wages (Matt. 26:6-13). Someone said, "We should not give from the top of our purses, but from the bottom of our hearts."

A Christian woman, a faithful giver for decades, came to church early one Sunday morning with her heart set on buying a new dress. When her husband's check had arrived Saturday, she had thought, "This one time I'll not put the tithe in the offering. I'll give only $1, and use the rest to buy that dress."

That Sunday morning she was on the committee preparing the elements for the communion table. As she started to fill the little glasses, the Lord began to speak to her about her plan to withhold the tithe. Feeling unworthy to take the Lord's Supper, she vowed to God that when she cashed the check, she would give the tithe to Him, and forget the new dress.

Later in the service, in sweet peace she partook of the elements which pictured the broken body and shed blood of the One who sacrificed all for us.

⋙ *Thoughtful Presents*   *March 14*

A little girl brought a bunch of handpicked dandelions to show appreciation to her schoolteacher. "These will fade," the little voice piped out, then added, "but you will smell forever."

According to one national PTA executive, a source of anxiety for parents of young children is giving presents to teachers. She advises against competing to give costly items, thereby embarrassing parents with limited income.

The PTA leader suggests getting the parents to donate toward a group present or a gift certificate. Or parents could give their children construction paper, crayons, scissors and glue to make a gift. Teachers seem to appreciate presents made by pupils themselves like cookies or artwork.

So, it's not their cost nor lavishness, but "it's the thought behind the gift" that gives them their value and significance. Perhaps picking dandelions isn't such a bad idea, even though they fade.

⋙ *Facing Death Victoriously*   *March 15*

A boy living in Idaho could never forget a lumber buyer named Benham who stayed a week in his folk's home. Benham was an outspoken atheist who denied the existence of any afterlife, heaven or hell.

Years later the boy, now a man, ran into Benham at a convention. The atheist, now 71, had an incurable disease. While hospitalized, he had been asked to be a witness to a deathbed will. He was mesmerized by the serenity of the lady patient who thanked him and said, "And now I am ready to leave this pain-wracked body to meet my friends who've gone before me and my Maker. Won't that be wonderful!"

Tears started down Benham's pale cheeks. "Look at me. I've nothing to look forward to, except to end in a pile of ashes. She, a believer, faces her final days with a smile. I would shove my hands into a bed of red-hot coals if by so doing I could secure a belief in a Supreme Being and an afterlife!"

"Where, O death, is your victory? . . . Thanks be to God! He gives us the victory through our Lord Jesus Christ" (1 Cor. 15:55-57).

≫ *March 16*   **A Little Child Shall Lead Them**

Outside Manila, capitol of the Philippines, stands one of the largest garbage dumps in Asia. It covers 74 acres, rises nine stories high, and is the length of three football fields. During the past 27 years, 60,000 families have built simple shacks in the dumpsite. In 2000 after monsoon storms, one side of a 50-foot mound of trash collapsed, burying 200 wooden shacks. More than 220 died in the mud landslide.

Immediately missionary teams responded with food, soap, clothing, and copies of John's Gospel. One church set up a school where children studied a Bible curriculum each weekday morning. As a result one nurse reported, "We have four-year-olds witnessing to their parents about how to be thankful to God even if they only have a little. Some of these adults have become Christians and leaders in the church."

≫ *March 17*   **Seeing the Sunny Side**

A farmer was whining, "My hay crop is a failure. What will I do?" A neighbor could see it was getting the farmer down, so he asked, "Is your potato crop a failure?"

"No."

"Your oats?" "No." "Your corn?" "Oh, no."

"Well," said the neighbor, "why not begin with thanks for your successes and put your failure last?" Doing so, the farmer's outlook changed for the better.

A thankful spirit helps us live above the circumstances. A Scotch believer, in mourning, thanked God "for 31 years' loan of Sandie, my dear son."

When afflicted from head to toe with a loathsome disease, Job was thankful for the day when his body would be raised from the grave and he would see God (Job. 19:25-27). His wife wanted him to curse God and die; instead he thanked God and lived—triumphantly!

Being thankful helps us to live victoriously.

⫸ *A Thousand Refugees* ⟍⟍⟍ *March 18*

Dr. Fred Scovel had been a Presbyterian missionary doctor in charge of a hospital in Tsining, China, in the 1930's when one day the city fell to the Japanese. The missionary compound was unmolested, its U.S. flag flying, a refuge for hundreds of people.

Six months later Dr. Scovel, beloved by all, was shot by a drunken, berserk soldier. At first his condition was in doubt, but by nightfall the crisis was over. Many refugees on the compound went to the pastor of the church next door and asked "Sir, may we go into the church? We would like to kneel down and thank the God who saved our doctor's life."

The church was opened the morning after the shooting. Though it was a weekday, more than a thousand people knelt to give thanks for saving their doctor's life. The pastor was back at work before many weeks and used this as an opportunity to tell again the story of Christ's coming to earth and giving His life for us all.

⫸ *New Morning—New Hope* ⟍⟍⟍ *March 19*

During World War II a journalist was looking around after a night of heavy bombing on a European town. Despite the wreckage around him, a beautiful day had dawned with blue sky and brilliant sunshine. He came to a small house. Its windows had been blown out by the bomb blasts, and the tiny garden was littered with roof tiles. At the door was a young mother with a baby in her arms. She stood there midst all the devastation.

The journalist stopped at the gate. "What a terrible night," he said. "Yes, but what a wonderful morning" was her reply. It was a statement of new hope, new possibilities, new beginnings.

A prayer in *The Book of Common Prayer* thanks God for His mercy and, "for thy preservation of us from the beginning of our lives to this day, and especially for having delivered us from the dangers of the past night."

≫ *March 20*   *Every Saturday*

Every now and again this item appears in *The Journal News*, a daily newspaper published in West Nyack, New York. "On Saturday, *The Journal News* publishes letters of thanks noting various acts of kindness, etc., in Rockland County. If you wish to note an individual or organization, please send your letter to us at the address in the Letters box on this page."

As far as Arthur Gunther, editor of the editorial page, can judge, this is the only newspaper in the United States that devotes a column exclusively to thank-you letters on a regular basis.

Since 1987 five or six thank-you letters have appeared every Saturday without fail. Some letters are thanks for support of various causes, like a 3-Day Walk for Breast Cancer, for hospital care, or help in an emergency.

Letters have even arrived from visitors from other countries for an act of kindness experienced when visiting the area.

≫ *March 21*   *An Ingrate*

Tom Brokaw's *A Lost Generation* has brought to light a host of moving World War II stories. Here are two other stories which illustrate contrasting responses to heroic acts.

In the thick of battle a young captain spotted a seriously wounded sergeant. Risking his life, the captain ran out and dragged the sergeant to safety. Hit by enemy fire, the captain later died. But the sergeant recovered. Home after the war he was entertained as guest of honor in the home of the captain's parents. Arriving late, half intoxicated, the sergeant acted like a boor.

Wolfing down a full course dinner, he hurried away after the meal with never a word about the man who had died to save his life. The mother burst into tears, sobbing to her husband, "To think that our son had to die for an ingrate like that!"

How different is the second story related in tomorrow's devotional.

≫ Annual Thanks   *March 22*

Every year an army major living in Los Angeles sent a message of thanks to a sergeant in Brooklyn. One day during World War II the major, bleeding from four shrapnel wounds, and his sergeant were trapped in a living inferno. Enemy shells exploded in front of them. An American barrage rained death-dealing steel to the rear. Though ordered to save himself, the slightly-built sergeant half-dragged, half-lifted the wounded major over a parapet and no man's land to a German dressing station. The major was given first aid. Both were taken prisoners and released at the end of the war.

"Every minute I have lived since that day of terror I owe to the sergeant," said the major. "Each year, on the anniversary, I repeat my appreciation by sending a letter of thanks."

≫ Two Unnecessary Years   *March 23*

In ancient Egypt, Joseph's prison stay on false charges by Potiphar's wife totaled about five years. But the last two years may not have been necessary had gratitude been exercised sooner.

One day Joseph correctly interpreted the dream of a fellow-prisoner, Pharaoh's chief cupbearer, predicting that the cupbearer would be restored to his former position. Joseph begged the cupbearer, "But when all goes well with you, remember me and show me kindness; mention me to Pharaoh and get me out of this prison" (Gen. 40:14).

"The cupbearer, however, did not remember Joseph; he forgot him" (40:23). He later rectified his neglect of gratitude, becoming the means of Joseph's elevation to second-in-command in Egypt, enabling him to save his brothers and father Jacob in the ensuing famine. But thanklessness kept Joseph behind bars for two unnecessary years.

» *March 24*   **Proper Boasting**

Some people boast about their wealth or honors, forgetting these could be stripped away in a few hours, or left behind at death.

A boaster who came to quick humiliation is Nebuchadnezzar. When Babylon was excavated centuries after his reign, over a million bricks were found with Nebuchadnezzar's name and title stamped on them. Once walking on the roof of the royal palace of Babylon, he had boasted, "Is not this the great Babylon I have built as the royal residence, by my mighty power . . ." (Daniel 4:30). But soon after he was stripped of his kingdom and forced to live for a year like a beast among the grasses.

The Bible says that the wise man should not boast of his wisdom, strength or riches, but rather of knowing the goodness of God (Jer. 9:23-24).

Whenever former champion mile runner Gil Dodds was asked to comment after winning a race, he used to say, "I thank God who helped me."

» *March 25*   **Really in the Know**

Analyzing the composition of the early church at Corinth, the apostle Paul noted that among the believers there were not many wise, influential, or noble persons (1 Cor. 1:26).

But he did not say, "Not any." Through the centuries some noble and wise people have believed. But as a rule, spiritual truth has been revealed to the unimportant and hidden from the VIPs who fail to seek God.

It's possible to know about rocks but not to know the Rock of

Ages; to know about flowers but not to be acquainted with the Rose of Sharon; to understand about light but not to follow the Light of the world; to trace the planets in their courses but not to know the Bright and Morning Star; to grasp the philosophies of the world but not to accept Him who is the Truth.

Jesus was thankful we don't have to be in Who's Who to know what's what! (Luke 10:21).

≫ Faith, Love, and Hope   *March 26*

A thanksgiving opens almost all of Paul's letters. In 1 Thessalonians he says, "We always thank God for all of you, mentioning you in our prayers. We continually remember before our God and Father your work produced by faith, your labor prompted by love, and your endurance inspired by hope in our Lord Jesus Christ" (1:2-3). The King James puts it, "your work of faith, and labor of love, and patience of hope."

This is the first mention in the writings of Paul of this famous triad of Christian virtues. The order is chronological, as faith began in the past, love acts in the present, and hope looks to the future.

Paul is also thankful for the widespread report and example of "how you turned to God from idols [work of faith] to serve the living and true God [labor of love], and to wait for his Son from heaven" [patience of hope] (1:9-10).

≫ My Refuge and My Fortress   *March 27*

A missionary in charge of a West African school wrote, "One evening while the children were playing on the swings I heard them screaming and discovered a viper only a few feet away. A few days previous we killed a giant scorpion just outside the kitchen door. A small puff adder, an extremely poisonous snake, was killed in our living room. In each case we paused to thank the Lord for his protection."

How often David poured out his gratitude for protection of

Thanks!

his life. After the Lord saved him from the hand of King Saul, David sang, "He is the God who . . . saves me from my enemies. You exalted me above my foes; from violent men you rescued me. Therefore I will praise you among the nations, O Lord" (Ps. 18:47-49). Dwelling in the shadow of the Almighty, David said of the Lord, "He is my refuge and my fortress, my God in whom I trust" (Ps. 91:1-2).

❧ *March 28*　　　　　　　　　　　　　　　　*A Good Friend*

A classic example of friendship in the Bible is that of Jonathan and David. After Jonathan's death, David in thankful memory elevated Jonathan's lame son, Mephibosheth, to his royal table for life (see 2 Sam. 9:1-13).

Perhaps you have a dear, close friend to whom you can say,

"Thank God for you, good friend of mine,
Seldom is friendship such as thine;
How very much I wish to be
As helpful as you've been to me—
Thank God for you!
"Some day I hope to stand
Before the throne of God's right hand,
And say to you at journey's end,
'Praise God, you've been to me a friend'—
Thank God for you!"

—Author Unknown

❧ *March 29*　　　　　　　　　　　　　　　*My Wife's Favorites*

"God grant me serenity to accept the things I cannot change, courage to change the things I can, and wisdom to know the difference. Living one day at a time, enjoying one moment at a time. Accepting hardship as a pathway to peace."

—Reinhold Niebuhr

"Lord, thank you for the snow and the wind and cold because

it makes us appreciate the spring and birds and flowers and trees more. Thank you for moving the table at work. I can get things easier. Thank you for my new boss. Amen."

—A mentally challenged girl

"O Lord Jesus Christ, who hast created and redeemed me, and hast brought me unto that which now I am; thou knowest what thou wouldest do with me: do with me according to thy will, for thy tender mercy's sake."

—A Prayer of King Henry VI

⋙ *Amazing Grace* — *March 30*

John Newton composed his own epitaph: "John Newton, clerk, once an infidel and libertine, a servant of slaves in Africa, was, by the rich mercy of our Lord and Saviour, Jesus Christ, preserved, restored, pardoned, and appointed to preach the faith he had long laboured to destroy."

In the midst of a violent storm in 1748 the Lord touched Newton's heart. When he applied for ordination in the Anglican church he was twice refused. Later accepted, for many years he led the parish at Olney where the attendance grew to 2,000. He became the main pillar of the evangelical party of England, and was influential in the conversion of William Wilberforce, a member of Parliament who helped abolish slavery in England. He also wrote over two hundred hymns. But the one that expresses best his thanks for God's mercy, still popular today, is *Amazing Grace.*

⋙ *Learning From Children* — *March 31*

Jesus told his disciples to become like little children (Matt.18:3). It is not childishness, but childlikeness that Jesus wants. As yet unADULTerated, children possess qualities which merit divine approval. Some of those traits:

Teachable. Adults often refrain from asking questions while children are not afraid to blurt out their ignorance, uninhibited and unembarrassed.

Forgiving. Adults often hold grudges to the next generation.

Unprejudiced. Until exposed to adult bias.

Frank. Adults put on airs, but should be more open, truthful with love.

Trustful. As children trust in the word of their parents, so God's children should have utmost faith in the promises of their heavenly Father.

Humble. Children don't have the pride adults often possess. To receive Jesus Christ, adults have to swallow pride, become like little children, admit their sinfulness and receive the gift of forgiveness.

Thankfully, adults may learn much from children.

❧ *April*

❧ *April Fools* *April 1*

An atheist complained to a Christian, "You Christians have all the holidays: Christmas, Good Friday, Easter, and others."

The Christian retorted, "You can have April first!"

A professed atheist asked why he should thank God for his food when he had earned it himself by working with his own hands. A Christian answered that to labor with his hands required health and strength and a body and brain capable of controlling physical coordination. Besides, he needed proper oxygen content in the air, and the sun to give healthful rays.

G.K. Chesterton, English novelist, said that the saddest moment in the life of an atheist comes when he knows himself to be thankful but has nobody he can thank.

❧ *An Encyclopedia for Thanks* *April 2*

A lady boarded a crowded bus. A man gave her his seat. She fainted. When she came to, she thanked him for the seat. He fainted.

The driver of a New York City taxi told how one of his morning fares had left a wallet in the cab with $200 in it. "I spent nearly two hours tracking the guy down. When I finally found him, he grabbed the wallet without saying a word. I didn't mind getting no reward or expense money for my time and gas. But he didn't even say thanks!"

The master of ceremonies of a radio program, "Job Center of the Air," found jobs for 2500 people, but only 10 thanked him.

Thanks!

When a mother was surprised at the arrival of a twelve-volume encyclopedia, the owner of an appliance store explained, "At our opening sale last week I gave away 400 gifts, but your daughter was the only one who wrote me a note of thanks. That set of books is for her."

≫ *April 3*   ***Guatemala's Presidential Award***

In 2000 Guatemala's President Alvaro Arzu awarded Paul Townsend the Presidential Medal for service to the nation's indigenous people, the Ixil.

Paul and his wife Sharon, missionaries under Wycliffe's Summer Institute of Linguistics, began living among the Ixil in 1974, translating the New Testament into their language, despite the difficulties of Guatemala's 36-year civil war.

The historic award was presented in the national palace where the President spoke from a clear-glass podium in a hall with thick, red carpet to an audience which included several missionary colleagues, government officials, and representatives from the Ixil. Draping a gold medallion around Paul's neck, the President concluded his speech, "Thank you for your contributions to Guatemala's indigenous people. It is my privilege to award you the Presidential Medal." Townsend shared the credit with all his partners.

≫ *April 4*   ***A Good Habit***

A boy was invited to lunch at a friend's house where the blessing was asked at every meal. The friend's mother asked the visiting boy if he could say grace.

"Sure," the boy replied, "grace." He thought it was a girl's name, for the blessing on food was never offered in his home.

Jesus gave thanks for bread and fish before performing His miracles of feeding the multitudes. Grace at meals acknowledges the divine bounties of sky, sea, and earth. The early Christians gave thanks at meals (Rom. 14:6).

A farmer entered a restaurant for his noon meal. He bowed his head and prayed. Four young city slickers nearby, to embarrass him, called out, "Hey, farmer, does everyone out in the country do that?"

Came the farmer's calm reply, "No, sons, the pigs don't."

Saying grace is a good habit for our generation to follow.

⇒ Praise From a Broken Leg   *April 5*

In Kansas a serious accident befell a young athlete on the all-Army track team, as he was preparing for a 400-meter hurdle race in the upcoming Olympic trials. He had run in both the 1988 and 1992 Olympic trials, and was hoping to make the next Olympic team in 1996.

In his own words, "As I approached the third hurdle, I knew that my steps were off. Though I cleared the hurdle, I took off a little farther than usual from the hurdle and cleared it. But when I landed and my hyperextended left leg bent inward to form what looked like the letter 'L,' I knew that it was a bad injury. My leg could not be repaired." Since his amputation God has opened numerous doors to give his testimony.

He says thankfully with Job, "The Lord gave and the Lord has taken away; may the name of the Lord be praised" (Job 1:21).

⇒ Double Happiness   *April 6*

In Dale Carnegie's well-known book, *How to Win Friends and Influence People*, a chapter, "If You Want to Gather Honey, Don't Kick Over the Beehive," suggests the value of genuine praise.

One girl who wanted to encourage her mother found opportunity at suppertime. Her mother had baked the best lemon pie she had ever made. After supper when she and her mother were doing the dishes, she put her hands on her mother's shoulder and said, "Mom, you always did bake a good lemon pie, but this afternoon you outdid yourself. This one was the very best. Thank you so much."

Thanks!

Her mother, surprised, took up her apron, wiped the tears from her eyes, and said to her, "You don't know how good it makes me feel to know that somebody cares for what I do."

G.K. Chesterton said, "Gratitude is happiness doubled."

≫ *April 7*   *Precious Possessions*

A man said to his neighbor, "After I was in the hospital last month, my outlook on things changed entirely. My stay there made me really aware of the most precious things in life." He paused, then, "Family, friends, and hospitalization insurance."

How thankful we should be for another precious possession in life—the use of our five senses, which bring to us the delight of sight, sound, taste, smell, and touch. One writer ecstatically exalts the fragrance of a blackberry bush, the scent of an apple, and the aroma of freshly baked bread.

A man on tour of a mental hospital met a woman soon to be discharged. She asked, "Have you thanked God today for your sanity?"

Babylonian King Nebuchadnezzar temporarily lost his mind and ate grass like the beasts of the field. On recovery he praised God for the return of mental health (Dan. 4:1-3, 33-37).

≫ *April 8*   *A Major Leaguer*

Former Atlanta Braves first baseman Andres Galarraga missed the entire 1999 baseball season while undergoing treatment for cancer. Bouncing back to a full return to the team the following year, Galarraga was one of the players voted by the fans to represent the National League in the 2000 All-Star game.

The Associated Press reported his appreciation. "I want to say thank you to all the fans that gave me great support last year and this year. I thank God for giving me my health and all the beautiful and happy things that have happened to me this year."

Perhaps you say, "My health isn't as good as it once was." Be grateful it is no worse. If you are not bedridden, thank God you can be up and around.

⇛ Freedom of Worship April 9

Every Sunday morning millions of people pass through open church doors to freely worship according to the dictates of their conscience. Any church bulletin lists a host of services for the coming week. Church doors are unlocked whenever we want to meet.

But there was a time when a church could not meet whenever it wished. The Christians of Rome used to meet in subterranean galleries outside the gates. The Church of the catacombs was a glaring contrast to today's Church of the open door.

About four centuries ago a multitude of Puritans, denied liberty of worship in their native England, sailed west to found the colonies of New England. Even today many parts of the world do not have liberty of worship. Sadly, many in the U.S.A. fail to avail themselves of this privilege. Jesus asked His followers not to stop meeting together. How thankful we should be for freedom of worship.

⇛ A Pastor's Yearly Salary April 10

The Bible of the Middle Ages could not be contained in one volume because it was printed on vellum far thicker than modern paper. Churches that possessed the Bible owned them in sections. Today pocket-size editions of the Bible are common.

The medieval Bible was in Latin, and only the most educated could read its contents. Because the book was a closed volume to most people, Luther and Tyndale translated the Bible into the language of the commoner. Since then, the complete Bible has been translated into more than 342 languages, parts into more than 2,000.

A Bible in 13th century England often cost an amount equal to $200 of our uninflated money. The price of a Bible once amounted to a minister's yearly salary. How grateful we are that today several copies are within financial reach of everyone.

Thanks!

Our Splendid God

A little lad flatly refused to say his prayers one night, insisting he didn't need one single thing in all the world. His mother suggested, "Suppose you give thanks for all the things you have." The idea pleased the boy who knelt down and gave thanks for his marbles, for his strong legs that could run so fast, that he was not blind like another boy on the block, for his kind parents, for his nice bed, and for many other things. His mother thought he would never finish. When he rose from his knees, he said, "Oh, mother, I never knew before how splendid God is!"

A contraction of the older word "worthship," worship is that activity which shows forth the worth with which we value something or someone. Saying thanks to God as the giver of every good and perfect gift is one way to express our recognition of His worth. Psalm 92 (KJV) begins, "It is a good thing to give thanks unto the Lord."

≫ *April 12* **God's Care for the Animals**

God's goodness is displayed in the animal world. He gives them means of protection. The bee has a stinger. The porcupine has its quills. And we all know the skunk's means of self-preservation!

God also provides coats for animals. They don't have to buy raincoats or jackets. And God provides food for them too (Ps. 147:9). No Shoprite or McDonald's for them.

At a busy intersection in New York City a 30-gallon can fell from a passing truck spilling milk all over the street. A policeman halted traffic while the driver retrieved the can. When he was about to blow his whistle for the "go" signal, he saw a small white cat creep out on the road and start lapping up the milk. He held up traffic, the light changing to green three times before the cat had drunk its fill.

Lord, "you give them their food at the proper time" (Ps. 145:15).

☞ *Treasure Above*   *April 13*

A sailor, shipwrecked on a south sea island, was captured, carried shoulder-high to a crude throne, and proclaimed king. According to their custom the king ruled for a year. The idea appealed to the sailor until he learned that, when a king's reign ended, he was banished to a lonely island to starve to death. Knowing he was king for the year, the sailor began issuing orders. Carpenters were to make boats. Farmers were dispatched to this lonely island to plant crops. Builders were to erect a home. When his reign ended, he was exiled, not to a barren isle, but to a place of plenty.

Jesus warned against storing up treasure on earth, instead urging us to lay up treasure in heaven (Matt. 6:19-20). It is not what we grab, but what we give out of a thankful heart that makes us rich. As Jim Elliot wrote in his diary before his martyrdom by the Auca Indians, "He is no fool who gives up what he cannot keep to gain what he cannot lose."

Thank God for the bank of heaven.

☞ *The Heidelberg Confession*   *April 14*

Question 86 of the Heidelberg Confession asks, "Why must we do good works?"

Answer: "Because Christ, after He hath redeemed us by His blood, also reneweth us by His Holy Spirit in His own likeness, that with our whole life we may show ourselves thankful to God for His blessing and that He may be praised by us then also that we in ourselves may be assured of our faith from its fruits, and by our godly walk may win our neighbors to Christ."

A lady in a hospital with polio became a Christian through the visitation of a minister. She was so grateful to the Lord for her salvation and full recovery that for 20 years she went back every week as a sunshine lady to the same hospital to visit and witness.

The mainspring of our obedience is appreciation of love divine that compels us to live for Him who died for us in a constant flow of thankful service.

≫ *April 15*   **Cure for Envy**

When the Queen of Sheba heard of Solomon's fame, she came to Jerusalem to see all his wealth, splendor, and wisdom. Overwhelmed, she said that his greatness far exceeded reports, and that the half had not been told. She could have been tempted to envy—to have a feeling of ill will at Solomon because of his vast superiority in so many areas. But instead she was thankful, saying, "Praise be to the Lord your God, who has delighted in you and placed you on his throne as king" (2 Chron. 9:8). It's rather hard to envy someone at the same time we're thankful for that individual. Gratitude is an antidote to envy.

A popular minister was perturbed when a famous preacher became pastor of a nearby church. Convinced that this orator would steal his congregation, he prayed, "Lord, I'll be thankful if you'll fill every seat in his church, and then send the overflow to me!"

≫ *April 16*   **The Best Yet to Come**

An elderly saint, seriously ill, told her pastor, "When they bury me, I want my old Bible in one hand and a fork in the other."

The pastor was caught by surprise. "Buried with a fork?"

She responded, "I've been thinking about the countless church dinners I've attended through the years. At those really nice get-togethers, when the meal was almost over, someone would come and say, 'You can keep your fork.' And do you know what that meant?"

The pastor still looked puzzled. She continued, "That meant dessert was coming! Not some cup of Jell-O, or little cookie. You don't need a fork for that. I mean the good stuff, like chocolate cake or apple pie. When they told me I could keep my fork I knew the best was yet to come!"

She concluded, "When they walk by my casket, I want them to turn to one another and say, 'Why the fork?' Pastor, that's when

I want you to say, 'She kept her fork because the best is yet to come!'"

⋙ *Thanks Changes Things* *April 17*

The night before He died, at the Last Supper, the Lord Jesus expressed thanks and sang a hymn. This attitude helped carry Him through the hours of agony that followed.

After a beating by the Sanhedrin, the disciples rejoiced "because they had been counted worthy of suffering disgrace for the Name" (Acts 5:41). Their Master had taught them to be thankful for persecution.

In jail with their backs bruised and bleeding from a cruel Roman scourging, Paul and Silas sang praises at midnight. Their thankful mind-set helped them endure the heavy load of pain.

Physicians at Johns Hopkins University discovered through psychological tests that people subject to fits of the blues took much longer to get over influenza than those with high morale.

Not only prayer, but also praise, changes things.

⋙ *A Missionary's Many Thanks* *April 18*

Message from a missionary after furlough from Nigeria:

"I give thanks to God for all of you who ministered to me during my home service: the chocolate-chip-cookie makers; the prayer warriors; those who opened their homes to me during my medical leave; those who brought meals to my house when my family came to Grand Rapids for Christmas; the World Missions office staff in Grand Rapids who helped in so many ways; those who put together a proposal for a new computer system for me; those who raised money for that system and gave gifts toward it; those who helped in setting it up and installing programs for the computer accessories; pastors who preached to my heart and who ministered to me and provided pastoral care . . . and the list could go on.

"Thank you, dear friends, for all your kindness. You have

been faithful in ministering to me in times of need. May our Lord and Savior bless and keep each and every one of you!"

≫ *April 19*   **A Missionary Asks for Patience**

From a missionary on arriving back in Nigeria:

"I am inundated by paper-work—whole cartons of it: various drafts of translation work-ups, minutes from committee meetings, 'to-do' lists, health records, financial statements, ministry records, and letters from all over. When I'm traveling a lot, papers get misplaced. It all piles up till I think I'll never dig my way out!

"What will heaven be like? Hopefully it means never having to deal with paperwork again! In the meantime, however, I am asking all of you who write to me to have patience. Your words of encouragement are precious to me. So, whatever you do, don't stop writing!

"For those of you who have sent gifts during the last few months for this ministry, I have begun writing notes to thank you. Lord willing, I will get 'caught up' during these few days in Nigeria. My thanks to all of you for your kindness and understanding."

≫ *April 20*   **Bunyan's Flute**

For three centuries John Bunyan's *The Pilgrim's Progress* sold more copies every year than any book except the Bible. A vivid allegory of the testings that confront the Christian, it has proven to be a reliable guidebook for pilgrims along the Christian way.

Strangely, the word, "thanksgiving" seems to be missing from Bunyan's vocabulary. But he does make reference to a place "Forgetful Green," and comments, "For if at any time the pilgrims meet with any brunt [vicious attack, blow, burden], it is when they forget what favors they have received and how unworthy they are of them."

During his long imprisonment in Bedford Prison, John

Bunyan carved a flute out of a leg of the only stool he had. With the flute he made melody and meditated on God's word. Because he had a thankful spirit he was able to pen this endurable writing.

≫ Gratitude   *April 21*

A 10-year-old boy left a note for his father under his dinner plate. His mother picked it up and read, "For cutting the lawn— $5." The mother left a note under his plate at the next meal which read, "For feeding and clothing you for ten years, and for loving you—$0."

Asked what contributed to his success, the owner of a very successful public relations company in Los Angeles answered, "Gratitude. While riding the bus to work in my early days I took the time to write thank-you notes to every person who had helped me in some way. I followed the practice through the years. It takes only a few minutes to write a thank-you, but reaps friendships for life."

We don't write thank-you notes to gain financial rewards, but, strangely, thank-you notes have a way of creating good will.

≫ Indescribable Sacrifice   *April 22*

A visitor to Australia wondered why his host walked with a limp, but he refrained from mentioning it lest the reason cause embarrassment. Finally, overcome by curiosity, the visitor asked the host's daughter if her father had always been lame.

"No," she answered. "That happened when I was a small child playing on the floor of the barn. I didn't know that a deadly snake was wriggling in my direction. Without hesitation my father jumped from the rafters. He killed the snake but he was hurt in the jump. He has suffered ever since, but he did that for me." The daughter's eyes moistened as she told the story.

In writing his hymn, "At the Cross," Isaac Watts wanted the vision of Jesus' sacrificial sufferings to "melt my eyes to tears."

Thanks!

The first letter in "thanks" is the form of a cross. Thinking of Jesus' sacrifice, Paul wrote, "Thanks be to God for his indescribable gift!" (2 Cor. 9:15).

≫ *April 23*   ***The Inside Latch***

Holman Hunt's art masterpiece, "The Light of the World," with exquisite coloring, blending of light and shade, and close attention to detail, is based on Revelation 3:20, "Here I am! I stand at the door and knock. If anyone hears my voice and opens the door, I will come in and eat with him, and he with me." Divine mercy waits on human hesitation. It's a call to decision—to open up to the Savior.

The painting portrays the door of the human heart, barred with nails and rusty hinges, overgrown with brambles and weeds. Jesus stands outside in the dark. The lantern's radiance falls on the door and reflects on Christ's face. His expression is appealing and tender. Thus He stands at the door of every person's heart, asking admittance.

In the painting the latch is on the *inside*. It is up to us to open the door, say "thanks," and enjoy His unimaginable blessings.

≫ *April 24*   ***Submarine Rescue***

Jesus prayed at the grave of Lazarus, "Father, I thank you that you have heard me. I knew that you always hear me . . ." (Jn. 11:41-42). Lazarus walked out of the grave. Jesus was grateful that He had a prayer-answering Father.

In the summer of 2000, one of Russia's newest nuclear submarines, the Kursk, crippled by a massive explosion, sank to the bottom of the ocean with 118 doomed men aboard. An earlier story with a happier ending tells of a British submarine disabled on the ocean floor. The sailors prayed. After two days of effort all hope of surfacing was abandoned. The crew, huddled together on the floor, kept praying. Suddenly a man fainted, lurching against a piece of equipment and jarring the jammed surfacing machinery into action. Soon the ship was nosing upward through the water which was to have been its grave. The jubilant sailors thanked God for answered prayer.

⫸ *Thanking Before Thumping* *April 25*

You cannot travel far into Paul's letters without finding a reason for thanks, often for signs of spiritual advance in the lives of new Christians. To the church at Rome he was thankful that their faith was "being reported all over the world" (1:8).

He was thankful for the many spiritual gifts in the Corinthian church (1 Cor. 1:4-7), and gave thanks to God for the financial contributions from the Philippians (Phil. 1:3-5; 4:15-16). Paul, along with Timothy, was grateful for the faith, love, and hope of the Colossians (Col. l:3-6). And he was grateful for Timothy's faith and for the faith of his mother, Eunice, and his grandmother, Lois (2 Tim. 1:3-5).

Too often we express criticism of new converts, instead of gratitude for their spiritual progress. Paul's letters did contain some corrective medicine, but only after noting their healthy points. He thanked before he scolded.

⫸ *From Bombs to Bibles* *April 26*

Captain Mitsuo Fuchida led the devastating attack on Pearl Harbor on Hawaii in 1941 and survived. Later, he survived combat in China. Six days before the Battle of Midway he suffered an attack of appendicitis. His next-in-command took charge and was killed.

Another day Fuchida was on the flight deck, waving pilots off, when an American bomb exploded and blew up the ship, throwing him into the water. Suffering two broken legs, he managed to float for two hours before being rescued. The day before the atom bomb was dropped on Hiroshima, he attended a military conference in that city.

After the war someone handed a tract to this Buddhist who

revered the Emperor as God. Reading the Bible led him to become a Christian in 1950. He returned to Pearl Harbor years later to preach at the Easter Sunrise service in Honolulu on "From Bombs to Bibles." He traveled as an evangelist, thankful to the Lord because He "spared my life so many times. I have dedicated the balance of my life to serving Him." He spoke in the church I pastored near New York City.

≫ *April 27*   *Replete with Thanks*

During a midweek church testimony meeting, one parishioner innocently exclaimed, "I've heard every sermon preached in this church for the last 50 years. But I've got a lot to be thankful for, 'cause I'm still a Christian."

Another testified she was thankful she could hear the alarm that went off early because it meant that she was alive. She also thanked the Lord for the person who sang off-key, because that meant she could hear. Security guards for New York City buildings near ground zero said before the attack on the World Trade Center that people passed by without looking at them. Now they say, "Thanks for being here."

Shakespeare in *King Henry VI* wrote, "O Lord! That lends me life, lend me a heart replete with thankfulness." The Psalmist vowed, "O Lord my God, I will give you thanks forever" (30:12).

≫ *April 28*   *Faithful Members*

It was my privilege to serve the same church 40 years. How does a pastor survive 40 years in the same pulpit? By the grace of God and the support of a loving congregation. Thank God for countless, faithful workers, who served in many ways:

—as Sunday school superintendent for 29 years;

—providing a missionary map, and a stained-glass missionary window;

—spending Saturday mornings on the phone, inviting new

home owners in our county to our church (many came);
—placing a pitcher of water under the pulpit on Sunday mornings for 40 years;
—using artistic gifts and calligraphy for advertising pieces;
—reading the highlights of the Sunday *New York Times* to a paraplegic;
—using public relations expertise to help us grow;
—providing flowers for the pulpit area weekly for decades;
—seeking to maintain unity in the church, avoiding fireworks.

For all these wonderful, faithful members I will forever be thankful.

❧ Animals Say Thanks   *April 29*

Animals sometimes have more sense than humans when it comes to a thankful spirit. One Puritan preacher put it, "Kindness works even on a brute." Then he quoted the prophet Isaiah, "The ox knows his master, the donkey his owner's manger, but . . . my people do not understand" (1:3). These animals, considered some of the least intelligent of domesticated creatures, seem to gratefully acknowledge their master's goodness, whereas humans often forget the divine hand that feeds them.

James Russell Lowell, commenting on the sight of a goat kneeling down to eat grass, suggested that this posture indicated the animal's gratitude. Another writer hinted that the satisfied grunt of the swine in trough and pen constituted the animal equivalent to human thanksgiving. And the dog who wags his tail shows more gratitude than the human who fails to offer thanks.

❧ Heathen Say Thanks   *April 30*

When Jonah was thrown overboard on his disobedient sea voyage, the sailors sacrificed to the Lord in thanksgiving for the stilling of the storm (Jonah 1:16).

For the Persians it was a matter of deep honor to repay all

Thanks!

kindness. Those who did a favor for the king had their names inscribed on an official registry of "royal benefactors." When unable to sleep, King Xerxes learned from a reading of his chronicles that Mordecai (Esther's uncle) had been responsible for saving his life, it became incumbent on the monarch to see that Mordecai receive a reward. The king's gratitude led to Mordecai's exaltation and Haman's hanging (see Esther 6 and 7).

If unenlightened heathen frequently express gratitude, how much more should those who profess to be the Lord's followers do so?

≫ *Saved by the Letter "M"* *May 1*

Born in 1707, Selina, Countess of Huntingdon and a member of England's high society, became a distinguished supporter of evangelical piety. Losing all her children and husband before she was 40, she devoted herself uninterruptedly to the revival work of Wesley and Whitefield.

Selina opened her house on Park Street, London, for preaching services. Her social connections in upper society drew many of high rank, including Bolingbroke, Chesterfield, and royalty. When a new primate of the Church of England introduced notoriously wild parties into the palace, she wrote a strong letter of protest to the king who stopped the improprieties. She sold all her jewels to build several chapels.

She often expressed thankfulness for the letter "m." Referring to 1 Corinthians 1:26 that not MANY noble are called, she explained, "Had it said, 'not ANY,' I could not have been redeemed. I was saved by the letter 'm.'"

≫ *The Crime of Owning a Bible* *May 2*

Imagine people arrested because they had a Bible in their home! This happened in England a few centuries ago. William Tyndale, a tutor in the home of a nobleman, noticed that the leading churchmen whom his master entertained were so ignorant of the Bible that some could not repeat the Ten Commandments. Realizing that the hope of England rested in people reading the Bible for themselves, he translated the New Testament into English. Because it was against the law to have a Bible, he found it necessary to print Bibles in Europe and ship them over to England, camouflaged in bales of cotton and other merchandise.

The bishops confiscated and burned all they could find. Tyndale was betrayed by a treacherous friend and burned at the stake. Be thankful for our freedom to own a Bible!

≫ *May 3*   *A TV Program Shows Thankfulness*

On *Who Wants to Be a Millionaire*, a recent popular TV quiz program, a contestant could win a million dollars by successfully answering 15 questions. As the questions proceed, the winnings rise. When the contestant is faced with a difficult question, three lifelines are available, one of which is to ask the audience to vote on the correct answer. Now and again the audience gets it wrong, but usually the audience bails the contestant out of potential elimination by picking the right answer. And almost always the contestant shows gratitude by waving to the audience, often with lips mouthing "thanks."

The contestants were acting properly in expressing their appreciation to the audience, for in many cases it resulted in winning a larger amount of money. But regardless of monetary gain, we should be quick to say thanks to others for favors bestowed.

≫ *May 4*   *Some Unusual Graces*

One steaming July day with guests for dinner, a mother asked her four-year-old girl to give the blessing.

"What should I say?" she asked.

"What you've heard me say, dear," mother answered.

Obediently she bowed her little head and out came, "Oh, Lord, why did I invite these people over here on such a hot day as this?"

A little boy, told to say the blessing, asked his father for help. His father prompted him. The little fellow nodded, then solemnly said, "Bless the hands that repaired this food."

The young daughter of a radio announcer, asked to say grace at the family dinner, bowed her head and said in a clearly enunciated voice, "This food comes to us through the courtesy of Almighty God."

The habit of grace, filtered through the innocence of children, may issue in some humorous petitions, but it's a habit worth instilling and perpetuating.

⋙ Daily Bible Reading   May 5

Elizabeth Montgomery, a free-lance writer in Edmonton, Canada, tells how at age 13 she began her mother's habit of reading the Bible daily. A special occasion years later showed her the value of her longtime practice.

It was the day before Christmas. Her father died at 5 a.m. that morning. After leaving the hospital, she went home to deal with her emotions. She reached for her Bible, her daily habit. In her own words, "I wondered how God could comfort me—surely the reading would be about the birth of Christ, rather than about the death of someone I loved. God surprised me, giving delight in my sorrow as I read from the Gospel of Luke, 'Sovereign Lord, as you have promised, you now dismiss your servant in peace. For my eyes have seen your salvation' (Luke 2:29-30).

"How I thanked God for the delight of daily Bible reading."

⋙ Her First Thank-You Note   May 6

William Stidger, a long-time respected professor at Boston University, reflecting on the great number of unthanked influences in his life, recalled a schoolhouse teacher who had gone the second mile in creating in him a love of poetry. So he wrote a letter of thanks to her.

A reply, scrawled in the weakness of age, read, "My dear Willie. I cannot tell you how much your note meant to me. I am in my eighties, living alone in a small room, cooking my own meals, lonely and like the last leaf of autumn, lingering behind. You will be interested to know that I taught school for 50 years and yours is the first note of appreciation I ever received. It came on a blue-cold morning and cheered me as nothing has in many years."

Stidger wept over that reply. Recalling others who helped shape his life, he wrote several similar letters.

Do you remember someone who significantly influenced the direction of your life: teacher, friend? It may not be too late to say thanks.

≫ *May 7*   *A Doctor Appreciates America*

A White Plains, New York, ophthalmologist recently returned from the Dominican Republic where he was a member of a team of American doctors working five straight days from 8 a.m. to 8 p.m., performing corrective eye surgery on 108 children and young adults.

Pointing to the happy faces in his photos, the doctor said, "They're overjoyed, because a cross-eyed child in a Third World country is seldom corrected. It's viewed as a disgrace to the family. These kids are not sent to school. They will be the last to be fed. Sometimes the family even cripples these kids so they can use them as beggars."

He has averaged one trip a year during the past three decades, paying his own way to poor countries where medical care for most people is nonexistent. He's always excited to get back home. He says, "I'm so thankful. I wonder how anyone can knock America."

≫ *May 8*   *Laws Against Worship*

When the Puritans sailed to the New World to seek freedom of worship, those left behind who failed to conform to the established Church of England suffered under four outrageous acts of Parliament, passed between 1661-1665.

The Act of Uniformity, aimed at ministers, prescribed forms of worship. Over 2,000 nonconforming ministers lost their pulpits. The Act of Conventicle forbade attendance at any religious meeting not authorized by the state. Penalties were severe. The Corporation Act, pointed at laymen, excluded Nonconformists from holding any public office anywhere in the entire country. The Five-Mile Act prevented any Nonconformist minister from coming within five miles of any place where he had pastored. Many good ministers were torn from their homes and lost their livelihood.

Let's thank God no such suffocating religious laws exist in our nation.

⁂ The Voice of Thanksgiving   *May 9*

Many Psalms urge gratitude. Psalm 100 (KJV) says, "Make a joyful noise unto the Lord . . . come before his presence with singing . . . . Enter into his gates with thanksgiving, and into his courts with praise: be thankful unto him, and bless his name." God's people are to publish his wondrous works "with the voice of thanksgiving" (Ps. 26:7, KJV).

Revival times seemed to bring a resurgence of singing. At the restoration of the Temple and walls of Jerusalem, the descendants of the musical groups were called on to lead the worship (Neh. 12).

One prime fruit of a Spirit-controlled life is to "Sing and make music in your heart to the Lord, always giving thanks to God the Father for everything, in the name of our Lord Jesus" (Eph. 5:18-20).

Would not much of our "tongue" trouble—criticism, gossip, complaining—diminish, if we used our lips more for thanks praising.

⁂ The Hound of Heaven   *May 10*

Man doesn't seek God, but God seeks us. When Adam disobeyed God, Adam hid, but God came asking, "Where are you?" We didn't beg heaven for a message, but God gave us the Bible. We didn't ask for a Savior, but God sent His Son. It's always been that way.

It was Jesus who sought Zacchaeus. Though Zacchaeus climbed a tree to get a good look at Jesus, the tax collector had no intention of stopping Jesus. It was Jesus who spoke first, inviting himself to Zacchaeus' home. It was while persecutor Saul was on his way to imprison saints in Damascus that Jesus stopped him in his tracks.

How thankful we are when we realize that it is "The Hound of Heaven" who has been seeking us. We love Him because He first loved us.

» *May 11*   ***Conversion Experiences***

A conversion need not be dramatic. Those reared in Christian homes are not so likely to have flamboyant conversions.

Conversions need not be uniform; no cookie-cutter standard is required. Though faith in Christ is the only way to God, there are as many ways to Christ as there are people. That's why conversion stories can be so interesting. And we're thankful for the variety.

Conversions may occur unobserved by others, though eventually its effects should work into one's outward life, and be noticed. No one sees the wind, but its effects are observable.

Conversions need not be sudden. Few will experience a conversion as dramatic as Paul's on the Damascus Road. For many, prior time involved in instruction and conviction may make conversion seem like a gradual experience.

A conversion does not transform a person completely. After birth comes maturation; after new birth comes spiritual growth.

Thank God that He loves us, knows us, and treats us as individually unique people!

» *May 12*   ***No One Else Knows the Language***

Shortly before China fell to Communism, Bob Pearce of World Vision shared a room in Shanghai's China Inland Mission quarters with a stranger who sobbed out his story. Twenty-five years before, he and his bride had come as missionaries. At their request they were sent to the Tibetan border, coming back to the coast once every three years for physical checkups and a re-stocking of dwindling supplies.

They worked seven years without a convert, though they had learned the language. In their seventh year God gave them a baby. The first convert was won through their little girl's ability to quote Bible verses in Tibetan. Now after 21 years there were eight converts. The man then told Pearce that at that moment his wife and 14-year-old daughter were on their way to America—his daughter had leprosy.

Asked why he wasn't going too, he said, "What about the eight struggling converts? I must return to Tibet. No one else knows the language." Next morning when Pearce saw him heading for Tibet all alone for three more years of separation, he bowed his head in wonder and thanks at such dedication.

⫸ Roses in Winter   *May 13*

The memories of happy days can temper the difficulties of the present. Some anonymous doggerel puts it this way:
> There was a dachshund once, so long he hadn't any notion
> How long it took to notify his tail of his emotion.
> And so it happened, while his eyes were filled with sadness,
> His little tail went wagging on because of previous gladness.

One man recovering from a bout with pneumonia was complimented on his fine spirit. He beamed in reply, "My sickness has been a blessing for I have had an opportunity to think over the wonderful things that have happened in my life and to remember all the good people I have known."

God gave us memories so we could have roses in winter.

⫸ Thank God for the Brightness   *May 14*

A pastor asked a lady how she was feeling. She replied, "I've got a terrible headache, but praise the Lord I've got a head to ache!"

Thanks!

A boy went to visit an uncle, an invalid for months in constant pain with cancer and totally blind. The boy, unused to the sight of suffering, never forgot the uncle's pinched face. But more vivid was the memory of the trembling man's words, "I cannot see you. But, thank God, I can hear you."

During the Welsh revival, a miner was converted. Fellow workers, wishing to test the reaction of a new convert, stole his dinner pail. Expecting an angry retort, for the convert had been known for his profanity, they were surprised when he smilingly replied, "Praise the Lord! I've still got my appetite. They can't take that!"

To cultivate perennial praise however bleak the way, remember there is always a brightness for which to thank God.

⇛ *May 15*   *Someone's Trouble Is Another's Thanks*

Someone imagined Sherlock Holmes and Dr. Watson camping. In the middle of the night Holmes awakes and nudges his faithful friend. "Watson, look up and tell me what you see?"

Watson: "I see millions of stars."

Holmes: "What does that tell you?"

Watson: "Astronomically, it tells me there are millions of galaxies. Theologically, that God is all-powerful. Meteorologically, that tomorrow will be a beautiful day. What does it tell you, Holmes?"

Holmes: "That someone has stolen our tent!"

A man cursed the pouring rain. Nearby a desperate farmer, praying for his fields of grain, thanked God.

An inconvenience to one person may cause gratitude in another.

⇛ *May 16*   *Flight Instructor From Above*

On August 5, 2000, Henry Anhalt, who had never piloted a plane, took control of the single-engine Piper he and his family were in, and landed it safely on a Florida airport after the pilot passed out at the controls. The pilot and owner of the plane,

Kristopher Pearce, was transporting Anhalt, his wife, and three sons back from teaching in a Daily Vacation Bible School mission in the Bahamas. Suddenly Pearce slumped unconscious over the controls. Using the plane radio, Anhalt happily made contact with a part-time flight instructor in the area who managed to guide him to nearby Winter Haven airport. The plane landed with minor damage. No one was injured. An autopsy showed that the pilot, age 36, suffered from coronary disease.

Anhalt, appearing on NBC's *Today* program, said that God "sent a flight instructor—you don't get much more help than that."

One news account began, "A family returning from a missions trip is giving thanks to God after a brush with death."

≫ *By Life or by Death*   *May 17*

In December 1934, John and Betty Stam, newlywed missionaries under the China Inland Mission, and parents of a baby girl, were attacked by communist soldiers in their home in Shanghai and placed under heavy guard. Allowed to write his superiors, John explained the circumstances of their capture, and sensing their grave danger, ended the letter, "May God be glorified whether by life or by death."

The next day they were forced to make a grueling march, stripped of their outer clothes, paraded through the streets, and executed. Their baby was delivered into the care of another missionary couple and brought back to America. Their martyrdom inspired many young people to dedicate their lives to missions, and the year 1935 saw the greatest amount of money contributed to the China Inland Mission since the crash of 1929.

We are moved by their thankful outlook, whether life or death.

≫ *So Many Ways*   *May 18*

Many are the ways to say thanks: leaving a generous tip when a waitress gives us good service; bringing or sending a gift to a friend or hostess; expressing it verbally or writing a note.

Thanks!

A little boy in Providence, Rhode Island, sent this message to the *Evening Bulletin*, which gave it prominent display: "Dear Sir: I prayed to God to make my mother get better and I want to thank God so when He reads the paper He can see it. From a little boy who loves God. May God thank you."

We had a friend who took a candy bar to her doctors every visit. On her 80th birthday she gave a special dinner in a lovely restaurant for her doctors and their wives, and presented them with monogrammed silver boxes. An avid rose-grower, during the rose season she takes roses to her doctors whenever they bloom, even between appointments.

We should express our thanks. And there are so many ways.

≫ *May 19*   **The Greatest Blood Donor**

Some years ago the phone rang late one evening in a home in California. "Mrs. Otto," a voice asked, "did you give a pint of blood to the Red Cross last December 14?"

Mrs. Otto learned that her pint of blood had saved a soldier's life. Said the hospital official, "He wants to thank you, but he leaves early in the morning for the East Coast."

A stunned Mrs. Otto made her way to the hospital. She learned that just before her blood had reached the makeshift clinic, the sergeant had been fighting for his life against terrific odds during leg amputation. When he regained consciousness the doctor handed him the tag from a blood container and said, "It was this woman's blood which saved your life!" Clutching the tag, the solder had muttered through clenched teeth, "Maybe—some day—I can thank her—for saving my life!" As he told the story he wept unashamedly. Mrs. Otto wept too.

Let's not forget to thank the greatest blood donor, Jesus.

≫ *May 20*   **You Never Said It Before**

An elderly mother was bedridden, and she called her three children to her bedside. Conscious but weak, the mother smiled wanly at their presence. One of her sons bent over and said, "You've been a good mother."

With a sigh the mother whispered, "Do you mean that?"

"Of course you have," all three children joined in.

The mother's voice came again, very faintly, "I didn't know. You never said it before, and I didn't know."

King Lear in Shakespeare sighed, "How sharper than a serpent's tooth it is to have a thankless child." Many children do honor their mothers. A college graduate at his commencement exercises walked to where an old lady sat. Kissing her wrinkled brow, he said, "Mother, that's your diploma. You earned it. Thanks for all you've done."

⇛ A Mother's Scars   *May 21*

On a school excursion on the Hudson River with parents along, a pretty freshman, circled by admirers, noticed walking along the deck a woman whose face was badly scarred. It was her mother.

Someone said to the girl, "Look at that pitiful old woman. Who is she?" The girl replied, "I don't know who she is." Unknown to the girl, her mother overheard the remark and kept walking down the deck.

At home that night, the mother took her daughter aside. "You've asked me so many times about my scars. I am going to tell you now something that I never told you before. When you were a baby, I had washed your clothes and was hanging them in the backyard. Suddenly the house burst into flames and I ran in to your little crib and gathered you up and lifted you out. I fought the flames. Not a hair on your head was singed, but I got these scars."

By that time the 14-year-old was in tears. "Oh, mother, I'm so sorry. I never knew." And she thanked her over and over.

Jesus today bears scars because of us. Have you thanked Him?

Some months after joining the Air Force, a young fellow placed a 1,000-mile phone call to his Christian wife's godly aunt. Though not a Christian himself, he begged his aunt, "Pray for me! Tonight I make my first jump! I'm number two! I don't want to worry my wife! I jump around midnight!" The aunt promised to pray.

Near midnight she slipped to her knees. At 1,000 miles south a huge bomber climbed up into the pitch black. No light shone inside or outside. Suddenly a green bulb flashed, the signal for paratrooper number one to jump. Terrified, he begged off. Number two, unafraid, fumbled for the door. He could feel the big bomber tilting. Through the doorway he went. As his parachute opened, a deafening roar ripped the night silence as streaks of fire shot through the sky. The plane crashed, killing every crewmember and paratrooper. Just the lone airman—number two!—escaped.

On furlough he professed Christ in a Wisconsin church and publicly thanked the Lord for answered prayer.

Paul also thanked God for escape from deadly peril (2 Cor. 1:9-11).

On his second missionary journey Paul endured much conflict in proclaiming the gospel in Thessalonica. He often wondered if Satan had destroyed the fruits of his labors. Paul's anxiety was real. New believers can be weak. Had tribulations caused some Thessalonians to renounce their faith? He sent Timothy to find out.

What marvelous relief when Timothy returned to Corinth with the report that midst all their severe trials, the converts had remained firm in their faith! His fears had been unfounded! And there was more. Timothy related their affection for Paul.

Such tidings dispelled Paul's worries about the Thessalonians, and gave him the impetus to face his own persecution he was then suffering at Corinth. It was a major factor which gave him victory and empowered him to stay 18 more fruitful months in that city. No wonder Paul wrote, "How can we thank God enough for you in return for all the joy . . . because of you?"(1 Thess. 3:9).

❧ God's 911   *May 24*

London, England, where Charles Spurgeon preached to thousands every Sunday, was devastated by a major cholera plague in the 1850s. Because of his constant contact with the dying, he felt that it was a matter of time before he fell victim. He was near exhaustion.

One day as Spurgeon was returning from leading yet another funeral, he was riveted by a poster in a shoemaker's window with these words from Psalm 91: "Thou shalt not be afraid for the . . . . pestilence that walketh in darkness; nor for the destruction that wasteth at noonday. A thousand shall fall at thy side, and ten thousand at thy right hand; but it shall not come nigh thee" (vs. 5-7, KJV).

The impact of Psalm 91 on Spurgeon was electric and immediate. "I felt secure, refreshed, girt with immortality. I went on calmly with my visitation of the dying. I suffered no harm."

He gratefully acknowledged the shoemaker for placing those verses in his window. Someone suggested that Psalm 91:1 (911) is God's number for us to call in time of emergency.

❧ Friends   *May 25*

A newspaper columnist defined a friend this way: "When you're at the end of your rope, he'll be at the other end pulling you up. He'll give you a job when others give you a jibe. He'll look out for your welfare when others give you a farewell." C.S. Lewis thought that perhaps half of all the happiness in the world comes

Thanks!

from friendship.

Many people become Christians through a friend. Friend Philip brought Nathanael to Jesus. A man sick of the palsy was carried on a makeshift couch by four friends who lowered him through a hole in the roof to the feet of Jesus who both healed him and forgave his sins.

The apostle Paul escaped from Damascus when friends lowered him over the wall in a basket by night. During an uproar at Ephesus friends restrained Paul from rushing into the amphitheater filled with rioting idolmakers. In his letters Paul sends greetings to friends everywhere. He ends the Epistle to the Romans by mentioning 27 friends by name.

≫ *May 26*   ***Telling the Truth***

Don Landaas, member of the elite Marine Ceremonial Guard, was on helicopter detail at Camp David in May 1959 when President Eisenhower was entertaining England's Prime Minister Macmillan. He broke the rules by entering a helicopter, sat down, and began to pray. Caught, he was sent back to Washington for trial. His buddies advised him to say he was investigating a noise.

At his trial, Landaas, a devout Christian, told the truth, "I didn't go into the helicopter to investigate a noise. I went in because I wanted to pray." He was sentenced to 20 days hard labor, fined $50, and busted from first class to buck private. But because of his excellent record, two weeks later, Landaas, an accomplished accordion player, auditioned and joined the Marine Band.

Three months later when Eisenhower returned to Camp David for weekend talks with Krushchev, he was one of the musicians chosen to provide the music. He returned often to Camp David, a place he had been told he would never set foot on again. He flew up in one of the same helicopters he had previously guarded. In the following months he played for President Eisenhower and 20 other heads of states.

Said Landaas, "I am so thankful I told the truth."

≫ *Beautiful Strings* *May 27*

Violinist Mary Canberg, Juilliard graduate, concert soloist, college instructor, and teacher of many gifted musicians, started the Rockland County (New York) Youth String Orchestra in 1962. The impetus came when a 15-year-old girl, who, after playing in a concert, said to Canberg, "I never knew strings could sound so beautiful." The local Parks Board and Recreational Commission agreed to sponsor the orchestra. Canberg gave her services free.

ABC-TV featured the 25th anniversary of this orchestra which gave two concerts annually of the finest classical music. Age of players ranged from 8-18, leaving no generation gap. ABC-TV called the high level of excellence a tribute to the community and to the director.

Canberg received this letter: "I want to thank you for the beautiful experience of being in your orchestra. The amazing sensation one gets while making music with others is something indescribable."

≫ *Presidential Relief Mission* *May 28*

Two months after the mammoth December 2004 tsunami devastation of South Asia, former U.S. presidents Bush and Clinton traveled to ground zero in Indonesia where they described the destruction as unimaginable and promised survivors that more help would come.

On the second day of their relief mission commissioned by President Bush, they flew in U.S. military helicopters over a barren landscape that was once a patchwork of rice paddies to the village of Lampuuk, where the sole structure standing was a large white mosque. The village had 6,500 inhabitants before the tsunami. Only 700 people remained.

Both leaders were stunned and humbled. Clinton said, "It's

Thanks!

almost impossible to appreciate the scope of this if you haven't physically seen it." Bush, looking out of the helicopter, said he was counting his blessings. "In my own heart I was saying we're very fortunate people not to have to go through something like this."

≫ *May 29*   **Recognized by Nature**

A well-known verse reads, "He came to that which was his own, but his own did not receive him" (Jn. 1:11). Because the first "own" is neuter, while the second "own" is masculine, one translator has suggested this paraphrase, "He came unto his own creation, and his creatures received him not." The implication is that though rejected by His people, the Lord Jesus was acknowledged by lower creation. His own things endorsed Him, but His own people did not.

At His bidding, the wind went howling back to its mountainous caverns, and waves subsided. The fig tree withered at His word. Fish appeared at His beck and call. The wild colt let Him ride on his back. At His death the sun hid its face as though disassociating itself from the guilt of that hour. Likewise the earth quaked and rocks rent in cataclysmic recognition. Were not these signs that *nature* recognized the Lord Jesus as Lord of the universe? And if so, how much more should every *person* thankfully acknowledge his majesty?

≫ *May 30*   **Memorial Day**

In recent years Memorial Day ceremonies have slowly decreased, gradually crowded out by mall shopping, trips, and picnics.

For several years, precisely at 10 p.m. on Memorial Eve, the bells of every church in a small Pennsylvania town began to toll. Gradually the lights in every home, store, and automobile were turned off. All traffic ceased. Stillness enveloped the town. Then the people stepped out to their front porches and lit their candles.

By loudspeaker came a prayer from a clergyman, then a rifle salute followed by taps, then the singing of the "Lord's Prayer." The lights went on again. Cars began to move. But for ten minutes everyone had remembered the heroism of our military personnel.

The Book of Common Prayer has a prayer for Memorial Day which says, "Almighty God, our heavenly Father, We give thee thanks for all those thy servants who have laid down their lives for our country."

⁂ *Prayer of Thanksgiving for a Faithful Pastor*   May 31

The following prayer of thanksgiving was given at the funeral of Pastor James Montgomery Boice at the Tenth Presbyterian Church in Philadelphia in June 2000:

"We would give You thanks today for the life and ministry of James Montgomery Boice. Father, we give You thanks . . . that he was raised in a godly home . . . for his years of preparation . . . for his love to his wife and daughters.

"And Father, we give You thanks for his preaching of the Word which brought great blessing to Tenth Presbyterian Church and to listeners of the Bible Study Hour Broadcast . . . for his commitment to missions . . . to international students, the homeless, and those suffering from AIDS.

"And Father, we give You praise for His able defense of the great truths of the Reformation . . . that he did not suffer greatly nor for long . . . that we will see him again on the far side of eternity, glorified in Jesus Christ." (Offered by Dr. Philip G. Ryken, now pastor.)

✺ June

✺ *June 1*   *Funeral of Todd Beamer*

Todd Beamer was one of the passengers on United Airlines Flight 93 on 9/11 who attempted to overcome the hijackers and likely saved the White House from attack. At his funeral his dad, David Beamer, concluded his remarks, "So Todd, thanks for all you were while you were here. You certainly represented your family, your Christian brothers, your God and our country very well."

Then he prayed, "Almighty God, thank You for Todd Beamer …. Thank You again for Your precious gift, Your Son, Jesus Christ, who died for us. Heavenly Father, I have known what that meant, but it is only in these recent days that I have a little more understanding of how it felt. I thank You so much that our son, Todd, has the promise of eternity because of the gift of Your son…. Also we pray, Heavenly Father, that Todd's witness and his actions can be used to Your glory in the things that matter most."

Following the Amen, David paused and offered one last expression of faith. "I have one more thing," he said, "God bless America, and Todd, we will see you later."

✺ *June 2*   *True Thanks*

A farm family came home from church one Sunday, fully expecting the usual sumptuous dinner their mother always cooked. To their amazement they found nothing on the table except corncobs.

"No, I haven't gone out of my mind," the mother said. "I just wanted to see if you would notice the difference." Little thanks.

In the dark hours of World War II when the British Army was being evacuated from the beaches of Dunkirk, an English clergyman noticed a young boy frequently coming to his church to pray. One day the minister approached the boy. "I see you've been here five days in a row. Do you make it a habit of coming here, son? Is one of your family in the thick of it across the channel?"

"My father, sir," said the boy, and then added, "but he got home yesterday, so I came to say my 'thank you' to God."

The Lord says, "What I want . . . is your true thanks." (Ps. 50:14, NLT)

⁂ Boasting in the Lord   *June 3*

When Joseph was called out of the dungeon to interpret Pharaoh's dream, he did not say, "I have special ability to understand dreams. I'm great at it. Let me show you." Rather, he humbly stated, "God will give Pharaoh the answer."

When Samuel Morse, best known for inventing the telegraph and the Morse code, was an old man, telegraphers in the United States and Canada chipped in to have a statue made in his honor. On the day of unveiling, over 2,000 gathered to watch for Morse's message of thanks for their gift to come over the wires. Morse sent this message: "Glory to God in the highest. On earth peace, good will toward men." The telegraphers cheered wildly. The whole western world was honoring his feats. He could have sent something like this: "Look at what I did." But in his hour of honor, out of gratitude to God, he repeated over and over, "Bless the Lord, O my soul, and forget not all his benefits" (Psalm 103:2, KJV).

The Psalmist said, "In God we make our boast" (44:8).

⁂ Another Pair of Shoes   *June 4*

A British pastor was preaching daily in a cathedral in an Australian city. In the same hotel where he was staying was a guest who was in the area to lecture on spiritualism. Guests customarily left their shoes outside their door for overnight polishing. When the preacher looked for his shoes in the morning, they were not there. He heard a noisy altercation between the spiritualist lecturer and the hotel manager. Walking toward the preacher, the manager said, "I'm sorry to say that a thief got into the hotel during the night and stole all the shoes."

"Hallelujah!" said the preacher. "I have another pair." Turning to the spiritualist, the owner said, "I had intended to come to your lectures on spiritualism, but now I'm going to hear this clergyman preach. You have been abusing me and denouncing the hotel. And all this clergyman said was 'Hallelujah! I have another pair.'"

The owner and his family, and most of the hotel staff, came to hear the preacher and became Christians, all because the pastor expressed thanks instead of anger.

⤜ *June 5*   *A Little Help From God*

For the privilege of work we should be grateful—and thankful for a good's night rest after a day's toil. And we should be grateful for food and clothing. A little boy in a store with his mother was given a piece of candy by one of the clerks. His mother prompted him, "What do you say, son?" Quick as a flash the boy replied, "Charge it!"

Too many think their material possessions come from Visa or MasterCard, forgetting to thank their Heavenly Father. During their forty-year wilderness wanderings the Israelites were fed and clothed, and walked in shoes that never wore out (Deut. 29:5). God does provide for our material needs.

Halfway up a mountain road a curve opened a breathtaking view of ocean panorama. A sign read, "Lookout View—Courtesy of Hotel." Below the words someone had penciled in, "Plus a little help from God."

⤜ *June 6*   *Medicine a Millennium Ago*

Let's be thankful we didn't live a millennium ago. Here are some 10th-century medical remedies. One cure for a headache involved binding the stalk of the herb crosswort to the head of the patient with a red bandana. Baldness could be overcome by an application of ointment from the ashes of burned bees. Spider bites could be remedied by fried, crushed black snails. Shingles could be could cured from a potion from the bark of 15 trees.

An excessive build-up of blood was believed to cause illnesses. The removal of that "bad blood" played a major role in the medical practices of the year 1000. Standard methods included the sucking of leeches, the slicing of veins, and the poking of red-hot irons to different parts of the anatomy. Aren't we thankful we didn't live in A.D. 1000?

⇒ John Bunyan   June 7

In the 17th century the British Parliament forbade worship outside the Church of England. Thousands were fined or dispossessed, all because they had tried to worship according to their conscience. During this period and for such crimes John Bunyan was imprisoned.

One November evening this man of commanding personal appearance and vitality walked thirteen miles to a service in Bedfordshire. Many had come to an appointed house to hear this able, itinerant preacher. His occupation was that of a tinker. However, the authorities were present and warned Bunyan that if he preached he would be arrested. The people urged him to adjourn the service, thinking of his wife and four children. He went out into the fields to decide. Returning to the house he began to preach. Interrupted immediately, he was taken to jail where he spent most of the next twelve years.

We are thankful for the life of John Bunyan and for his classic, The Pilgrim's Progress, the enduring allegory of the Christian life.

⇒ Peanuts   June 8

Charles M. Schulz, cartoonist of the popular series, Peanuts, delighted the world with the adventures of Charlie Brown, his

Thanks!

friends, and a dog named Snoopy for nearly 50 years. The series eventually ran in 2400 newspapers, the most widely syndicated comic strip in history, reaching millions of readers in 68 countries.

His characters were quite human, wrestling with the adversities and foibles of life. One sociologist suggested that seeing ourselves in the strip made it powerful in our lives. One lady who had a "lousy" childhood said, "Faith in God plus the incredible humor, tremendous art and wise counsel of the Peanuts gang pulled me through many difficult moments." One preacher likened the strip to Jesus' parables.

Not only were his readers appreciative, but Schulz in his last strip wrote, "I have been grateful over the years for the loyalty of our editors and the wonderful support expressed to me by the fans of the comic strip."

<hr>

≫ *June 9*   ***The Prominence of Praise***

God's people broke forth in the song of Moses after the victorious crossing of the Red Sea (Ex. 15). But musical expression reached its height under the leadership of David, sweet singer of Israel, who not only composed dozens of psalms, but who arranged for a choir and an orchestra in the formal worship of the people. Entire personnel of the temple choir and orchestra totaled 4000.

At the dedication of Solomon's temple the choir, plus an orchestra including 120 blasting and blaring trumpets, sang and played together "to give praise and thanks to the Lord" (2 Chron. 5:12-13).

Praise was prominent in early church services. Thanksgivings were a common component (1 Cor. 14:16-17). Paul commanded believers to "teach and admonish one another...as you sing psalms, hymns, and spiritual songs with gratitude in your hearts to God" (Col. 3:16).

Thankfulness leads to worship, and worship to thanksgiving.

☞ *The Matchless Name* *June 10*

One morning a medical missionary in China, who always gave the gospel to those who came for help, noticed a woman, stooped with age, who had come a long way. Her heart opened to the Savior. She wept.

Weeks went by. One morning he again looked into the face of the old woman. She exclaimed, "Oh sir, He has saved me and I know He lives in my heart. He has made my life so happy! But, sir, I've forgotten His name. Could you please tell me His name again?"

The kind physician had the privilege of repeating over and over into the ears of the old woman the matchless name of Jesus. As he did, she kept echoing his name. After a while, the woman bowed, thanked the doctor, and headed back toward her village. He watched her disappear, confident that never again would she forget that name.

That story inspired Lela Long, in gratitude for the Lord Jesus, to compose the song, "Jesus Is the Sweetest Name I know."

☞ *Appreciation for God's Blessings* *June 11*

Mitch Glaser, Executive Director of The Chosen People Ministries, relates how hard it was at first to accept the idea of raising his own support when he became a missionary. He was horrified at the thought of asking other people for money. His parents were hard-working immigrants.

But he came to see that the process of raising support was a strong lesson in learning how to depend on the Lord, in providing givers a source of blessing, and in helping them meet a holy obligation. In the Old Testament, God provided for the Levitical priests through a temple tax, a system of peoples' willing tithing, and their animal and grain offerings. When the people walked with God, the priests were well taken care of.

Says Glaser, "I believe that true missionary giving—in fact, all giving to the work of the Lord, whether it be our time, treasure or talent—is the overflow of our thanksgiving to God for His blessings."

❧ *June 12*   *Basic Motive*

In his book *What's So Amazing about Grace?*, Philip Yancey says, "If I had to summarize the primary New Testament motivation for 'being good' in one word, I would choose gratitude. The apostle Paul begins most of his letters with a summary of the riches we possess in Christ. If we comprehend what Christ has done for us then surely out of gratitude we will strive to live 'worthy' of such great love. We will strive for holiness not to make God love us but because he already does."

For example, in his treatise on salvation in Romans, Paul begins with the reality of sin, then explains the marvelous redemptive work of Christ, resulting in our justification, sanctification, and ultimate glorification. And then in the final section he urges his readers to show gratitude for such love, "Therefore, I urge you, brothers, in view of God's mercy, to offer your bodies as living sacrifices, holy and pleasing to God . . ." (Rom. 12:1).

❧ *June 13*   *Sure Beats Caustic Criticism*

Well-known author Philip Yancey, after a spiritual checkup at 50, resolved, "to allow the good—the beauty of nature, health, kind words of others—to penetrate as deeply as the bad. Why does it take about 17 encouraging letters from readers to overcome the effect of one that is caustic and critical? If I awoke every morning and fell asleep each night, bathed in a sense of gratitude and not self-doubt, the in-between hours would doubtless take on a different cast."

On the first night of Billy Graham's crusade AMSTERDAM 2000, a sudden downpour fell on the participants waiting to board the trains to take them to the opening ceremony. Most began to grumble about getting wet. However, one woman from

Africa, who was dressed in her native garb, stood in the rain with her hands upraised. "Praise God!" she said. "I have not seen rain in three years!" No complaining for her—just joy and thanks.

≫ *Joel Sonnenberg*   *June 14*

Joel Sonnenberg at two years of age was burned on over 85% of his body when an 18-wheeler smashed into his family's car. After several months at the Shriners Burn Institute in Boston and 45 surgeries of facial reconstruction and skin grafting (he lost lips, ears, nose, fingers, toes), he draws shocked stares everywhere. I know—I was his pastor when this happened. He wears a cap to protect his skull. He comments, "How I look is who I am. And I'm content with that."

Though he has not mastered tying his own shoes, he has learned to excel beyond all expectations. In high school he was named to the all-conference soccer team as a midfielder. At Taylor University he was chosen by classmates to speak at his commencement. Joel has been featured in numerous magazines, spoken at major conventions, and appeared on many TV interviews, including *48 Hours* in 1999.

Thankfully he comments, "I get attention wherever I am, so I can have an impact on people, and God can have an impact through me anywhere."

≫ *Realizing Your Blessings*   *June 15*

Dale Carniege, author of *How to Win Friends and Influence People*, once in a deep depression from which he could not seem to extricate himself, did a strange thing. Assuming he had lost everything, he took a sheet of paper and listed each loss:

Broken in health
My wife has deserted me
I'm fired from my job
My money is gone
My children are all in jail

Looking at the paper he said, "There isn't a word of truth in it." Then he tore it up. He had realized his blessings.

Many psalms combine thanks and adversity. The Psalmist seems always to find a reason to thank, however dark the cloud.

≫ *June 16*   **Songs at Midnight**

In a Philippian jail after an unjust beating, Paul and Silas could have bemoaned their plight. Instead their thankful spirits prompted praises at midnight. The jailer, accustomed to prisoners spewing hate—certainly not singing psalms—was jarred as much by their attitude as by the sudden earthquake. The result— the jailer and his family believed and were filled with joy (Acts 16:25-34).

During a fearsome Mediterranean storm, Paul gave thanks for food and for safety. Sailors became cheerful, perhaps converts (Acts 27:21-44).

William Law, an 18th-century churchman, considered a thankful spirit the essential quality of sainthood; "Would you know who is the greatest saint in the world? It is not he who prays most or fasts most; it is not he who gives alms, or is most eminent for temperance, chastity, or justice, but it is he who is always thankful to God, who receives everything as an instance of God's goodness, and has a heart always ready to praise God for it."

≫ *June 17*   **Periods of Mental Illness**

Poet and hymnologist William Cowper wrote many popular hymns, such as "There Is a Fountain." He also gave English literature a number of minor poems and translations of Homer.

For a while Cowper practiced law, but then he began to suffer periods of mental illness. He had to be put under medical care in the "private madhouse of Dr. Cotton, a pious man," who helped Cowper many other times. Cowper's relapses were frequent. Tormented by fear of having committed the unpardonable sin, he suffered nervous breakdowns and made several attempts at suicide. He was often straightjacketed in an insane asylum for his own protection. When feeling well, he rejoiced in Psalm 118:29, "Give thanks to the Lord, for he is good; his love endures forever."

In his hymn "God Moves in a Mysterious Way," Cowper expressed gratitude for the Bible: "Let everlasting thanks be Thine for such a bright display."

⫸ A Child's Recovery   June 18

Though the beauty of written prayers does not impress deity, neither do verbosity, incoherence, nor meaningless repetition. Written prayers of others may genuinely express our inner desires, and give an impetus to our own praying, like this prayer from *The Book of Common Prayer*:

Thanksgiving for a Child's Recovery From Sickness:

Almighty God and heavenly Father, we give thee humble thanks that thou hast been graciously pleased to deliver from his bodily sickness the child in whose behalf we bless thee and praise thy Name, in the presence of all thy people. Grant, we beseech thee, O gracious Father, that he through thy help, may both faithfully live in this world according to thy will, and also, may be partaker of everlasting glory in the life to come; through Jesus Christ our Lord. Amen.

When Elisha raised the Shunemite woman's son from the dead, she "fell at his feet, overwhelmed with gratitude" (2 Kings 4:37, NLT).

⫸ The Barnabas Committee   June 19

One dismal morning a professor in his first year of teaching at a western Bible college, struggling with his workload, opened the class with an apology. Removing his glasses, he said, "I want to ask your forgiveness for my inadequate preparation over the last few weeks. Please pray for me." He replaced his glasses with shaking hands, sighed, and began the lecture.

At lunch several students decided to pray regularly for him

and for other professors also facing struggles. Because the apostle Barnabas was always encouraging someone, they called their prayer ministry, "The Barnabas Committee." They communicated their care with simple notes, anonymously sneaking around campus at night to deliver their notes to the doors of professors.

The profs, touched by this concern, sent thank-you notes to the campus post office which, not knowing who the group was, posted the notes on the bulletin board where everyone would read them. The entire student body began to encourage each other with notes, thank-yous, hugs, prayers, and comfort.

⚛ *June 20*   *A C T S*

If called upon to define prayer, most people would say, "It's asking God for things." One minister said, "Too many Christians try to put all their begs in one askit." Someone suggested an acronym to remind us that praying involves four components: ACTS.

Adoration. True prayer begins with awe. A man, watching a sunrise, said, "I see the glory of God. The whole earth is full of his glory." Prayer begins with reverently adoring God for his inexhaustible excellencies.

Confession. It's well to search our hearts for areas in our life that need cleansing, confess our transgressions, and assure ourselves of pardon through Christ's abounding grace.

Thanksgiving. We should never forget to thank God for his inestimable redemption. And it wouldn't hurt to pause and list off some specific benefits recently received instead of taking them for granted.

Supplication. Now we're ready to present our request list.

⚛ *June 21*   *Timbuktu*

For years Stephen Saint, whose father Nate Saint was killed by Auca Indians in Ecuador, thought that Timbuktu was a fictitious name. On a relief mission in Africa in 1986 he found out that Timbuktu was a real place and hitched a ride there on a six-seater

UNICEF plane from Mali. He was able to contact young Pastor Nouh, and an American missionary translator. Nouh told how when he became a Christian, his family condemned him as an outcast. Saint asked, "Where did your courage come from to risk your life?"

Nouh replied, "A missionary gave me a book about five young men speared to death, taking God's good news to stone-age Indians in South America." Turning to Saint, the translator spoke up, "Didn't one of those men have the same last name as yours?"

"Yes," said Saint quietly, "The pilot was my father."

"Your father!" Nouh cried. "The story is true!"

The three men talked for hours. Said Saint, "Time came to take the plane back. How thankful we were that God had arranged for us to meet at the end of the earth to encourage each other."

≫ *Handmade Gifts*   *June 22*

A columnist tells how she used to make her sisters gifts for Christmas—crocheted doilies, potholders, quilted pillows, or homemade jams. She started working on them in August. One year, instead of saying thank you, two of her sisters joked about how you could count on her to make a present instead of buying one. The columnist stopped making them presents.

When a sister mentioned she missed the handmade gifts, the columnist explained why she stopped. Her sister seemed surprised. "It was only a joke," she said.

The columnist replied, "If the joke had been accompanied by a thank-you, no one would have been offended. I couldn't know the gifts were appreciated if no one said it. I was left with the impression that my sisters thought I was cheap instead of thoughtful."

The columnist concluded, "I don't know about other people, but I'm a lot more likely to do a favor for someone who appreciates me."

⇒ *June 23*   ***A Double Thanks***

When Jesus instituted the ordinance known as the "Lord's Supper," the Gospel record states explicitly that He gave thanks twice, once before breaking bread and again before drinking wine. "While they were eating, Jesus took bread, gave thanks and broke it, and gave it to his disciples . . . . Then he took the cup, gave thanks and offered it to them" (Matt. 26:26-27). These elements pictured His crucified body and shed blood. The night before He died, with full knowledge of His imminent sacrifice for sin, He gave thanks for that redemptive death.

In relating how the Lord's Supper was initiated, which knowledge he received by direct revelation from the Lord, Paul mentioned the double giving of thanks, once before each element (1 Cor. 11:23-25). Paul also speaks of "the cup of thanksgiving" (1 Cor. 10:16). Paul was ever thankful—doubly—for the body and blood of Jesus.

⇒ *June 24*   ***A Pastor's First Congregation***

As a bride, my wife joined me in our five-year, first pastorate in a Pennsylvania coal mining town. We stayed for the first month in the unused home of a member. It had a coal stove, and we promptly smoked up the home. No complaint from the owner.

Neither dentist nor doctor ever charged us. Every Sunday night the local justice of the peace, who had lost both legs in an accident, read English poetry to us over generous bowls of ice cream. The former pastor and wife backed us 100%. Saturday nights a lady in her 80s delivered rice pudding. Members taught us the best markets and discount stores. One minister's wife mentored my wife in child rearing. She taught her when anxious, "Don't go to the phone, but to the throne." Another minister's wife said, "Use your best china and silver every day and you'll always be prepared for unexpected guests."

Thank you, Pennsylvania congregation, for teaching us love in action.

⇒⇒ "Miracle Joy" *June 25*

After a six-year struggle with infertility, Marsha Mark's doctor told her and her husband that they needed to accept the fact that they would never have biological children. Adoptive agencies considered them too old. Despite discouragement, Marsha had kept praying, but not her husband. Suddenly one day she didn't feel well. The infertility clinic gently turned down her request for one more pregnancy test, implying she really needed a therapist. Finally the clinic agreed. Next day her phone rang. "Your test came back positive." She made them repeat the answer six times. When she called her husband, he simply said, "Well, that's interesting."

Over the next 14 days the hospital requested four more pregnancy tests. Her full-term pregnancy was uneventful. Amanda Miracle Joy was born Oct. 12, 1996. Her middle names convey thanks for their miracle baby and a boost to her daddy's belief in prayer.

⇒⇒ He Taught Us How to Die *June 26*

In 1970 I learned that my dear friend, David Goodwin, once my Sunday school teacher and pastor, was seriously ill in East Moline, Illinois. His daughter, Sally, who had left her career as a concert harpist in New York City to take care of him, told me that his weight had gone from 180 to 90 pounds and that he preached his sermons from a wheel chair. His final series dealt with Peter's instructions in his second epistle, written in full awareness of his own imminent death. She said, "Dad wants you to conduct his funeral."

Three Sundays later word came that David had passed away. On awakening he said, "I'm going home today." Then he asked his daughter to read his favorite psalms.

Over 1200 came to pay respects. Deeply loved, he had pastored this church for 34 years. His daughter, with harp positioned beside the casket, movingly played his favorite hymn, "Safe in the

Thanks!

Arms of Jesus."

Members of his congregation commented, "We thank God that for 34 years Pastor Dave has taught us how to live. Now in these last few months we are thankful that he has taught us how to die."

June 27   *Missionary Wives*

Missionary wives have a rich tradition. Well known is the story of Elizabeth Elliot, wife of Jim Elliot, who was martyred by the Aucas. After his death she was able to gain entrance to the tribe.

In some of the most unreached places of the earth, these unusual women provide stability for their families, serving as teachers, health care providers, and evangelists for entire communities. One remarkable woman raised her children in an Indonesian village where she gathered rainwater to drink and had only a diesel generator for electricity. As a registered nurse, she became the town's only "doctor," delivering babies, treating everything from headaches to malaria. Naturally weary at times, she was motivated by gratitude to the One who left heaven for us.

A child near death was brought to her. She diagnosed his illness in time to save him. The boy's grateful father later became a pastor.

Thank God for missionary wives.

June 28   *Serving Through Her Novels*

From 1976 to 1985 Francine Rivers had a successful writing career in the general market, winning several awards. After becoming a Christian in 1986, she wrote *Redeeming Love* as her statement of faith. Since then, Francine has published numerous books in the Christian booksellers market, winning several awards and reader devotion.

She is writing five novellas on the women in the lineage of Jesus: Tamar, Rahab, Ruth, Bathsheba, and Mary. Some of these women made big mistakes, yet God in His perfect plan used these imperfect women to be the progenitors of the Savior of the world.

Building on the facts of Scripture, Francine creates action, dialogue, internal motivations, and, in some cases, additional characters she feels are consistent with the biblical record.

Through her work she wants to worship and praise Jesus—a thanksgiving for all He has done and is doing in her life.

⇛ *Godly Writings* *June 29*

Through the pages of Bunyan's *The Pilgrim's Progress*, many have been led to travel from the City of Destruction to the City of God. Edith Schaeffer stated that she was deeply influenced by this classic.

A book, *The Life and Diary of David Brainerd* (missionary to the Indians of New England in the 1740s), edited by the early American minister Jonathan Edwards, exerted a strong formative influence in the lives of many Christian leaders, including John Wesley, William Carey, Henry Martyn, Robert Murray McCheyne, David Livingstone and Jim Elliot.

C.S. Lewis, atheistic in outlook and teaching at Oxford, was influenced by the writings of George MacDonald and G.K. Chesterton. Many, including Chuck Colson, have been helped toward Christ through C.S. Lewis' *Mere Christianity*, to say nothing of the effect of Lewis' other writings. Colson, in turn, has written some significant books and made an impact on our prison system.

Thank God for godly writers and godly writing!

⇛ *The Thorpedo* *June 30*

At the 2000 Olympics in Sydney, much attention centered on a 17-year-old Australian swimmer, Ian Thorpe, who recently had broken the world records in the 200- and 400-meter freestyle.

He expresses his appreciation "in that I've been given a gift, and that I've realized what it is and I'm able to work on that." His size is definitely part of his gift. Almost 6 feet 5, at 215 pounds, and wearing a size 17 shoe, he has an extraordinary capacity for "aerobic exertion." He is able to shoot across a pool with a six-beat kick to every arm stroke. His nickname: "The Thorpedo."

In the Olympic competition he won the men's 400-free style. His countrymen may have been disappointed in his second-place finish in the 200-free style. But he swam a leg of the 400-meter men's relay, winning the gold medal, upsetting the U.S.A. which had never lost this event in the Olympics.

The Australian head coach says, "I go to bed at night and thank God that we have him. He could be the greatest swimmer ever." He did go on to win a gold medal at the 2004 Olympics in Athens.

❧ July

❧ Take Stock Often
July 1

At a banquet in New York City at which pork (forbidden in the Old Testament law) was the main dish, Daddy Hall, an Episcopalian rector and open-air preacher, prayed this blessing: "Dear Lord, if thou canst bless under grace what you cursed under law, then bless this bunch while they munch this lunch."

One little fellow explained, "In our family we hold hands while we say grace so nobody starts to eat."

A character in a Charles Dickens story said, "Not knowing at one meal where I shall get the next is a great help to thankfulness."

I shall never forget walking down a main street in downtown Amman, Jordan, and seeing a crust of bread sitting on a ledge of a church. The missionary explained, "Someone is so grateful for daily bread that either he has not eaten it all, or left a crust for some hungry person to find."

We need to take stock frequently, and thank God repeatedly.

❧ Instrument of Thanks
July 2

Man is the only earthly creature with the gift of speech. The tongue was meant to bless, though sadly the tongue incongruously spews out both good and bad. Our tongues should be an instrument of evangelism, edification, prayer and encouragement. Apt words provide the soothing balm of God's solace for the afflicted and bereaved. Also, our tongues can be an instrument of praise and thanksgiving. We were created to glorify God. In heaven the living creatures, joined by 10 thousand times 10

Thanks!

thousand give "glory, honor and thanks to him who sits on the throne" (Rev 4:6-9), saying with a loud voice, "Worthy is the Lamb, who was slain, to receive power and wealth and wisdom and strength and honor and glory and praise" (5:11-12).

May our tongues, here and now, flow with praise and thanks.

≫ *July 3*   *Door of No Return*

On a trip across Africa in 1986, my wife and I visited Goree Island, the best preserved slave center in Africa, just off Dakar, capital of Senegal. This westernmost point of Africa was the logical port for shipping slaves.

On the island stands the Slave House, an old stone building, for years used as slave-trading headquarters. When you visit here, a guide describes the ugly business of shipping slaves, how infants were crowded together in a tiny cell, how shackled men fought over the one daily plate of food, how they were loaded onto ships through a door of no return and into cramped positions in crowded quarters below deck. Once past the door—no way out. To jump was to be devoured by sharks.

One recent black tour group, about to leave and facing the door of no return, hugged each other in tears. And holding hands they thanked God for the strength of their ancestors, for their own freedom, and prayed for an end to all hate and prejudice.

≫ *July 4*   *"The Gold You Should Have Won"*

Canoeist Bill Havens was predicted a sure gold medal winner at the 1924 Olympics in Paris, France. When his wife became pregnant months before the games, he figured that she would likely give birth about the time his contest was scheduled. Though she maintained she could deliver in his absence, he considered the baby's birth too important to miss, so he stayed home for the birth of his son, Frank, on August 1, 1924. Of course, he often imagined what could have been, but he never expressed regret at his decision to stay home to be with his wife. In the years that followed he devoted his energies to his boy, concentrating on developing in him a love for canoeing.

When Frank was 28, the Olympic Games were held in Helsinki, Finland, and he was chosen to represent the U.S.A. in the canoeing event. The day after the contest, Bill received a telegram from his son that read, "Dear Dad, Thanks for waiting around for me to be born in 1924. I'm coming home with the gold medal that you should have won. Your loving son, Frank."

⇛ New York Times *Ad*   *July 5*

The Sunday *New York Times* (July 5, 1964) carried a most unusual piece, headed simply "Thanks." Almost a quarter-page, it cost nearly $1000 then. Eliezer Goldfarb, who came from a long line of rabbis, acting on his urge to say publicly that he was grateful for living in the United States, prepared a little essay in blank verse. Cost represented a fourth of his savings. Goldfarb's life had never been easy and not always happy. He was on the stage for many years, a member of the original cast of "Abie's Irish Rose," a Broadway hit in the 1920s. After the depression he was a salesman, then a doorkeeper at the New York City Center. "This last year has been such a wonderful year," he said. "The advertisement is to commemorate that and also as a memorial to my wonderful parents."

His short essay of 28 lines of blank verse, expressing his gratitude for being alive and for living in the U.S., was simply titled, "Thanks."

⇛ *One of the Finest Words*   *July 6*

It was once reported that Rudyard Kipling, England's Poet Laureate, received ten shillings for every word he wrote. It was also reported that some students at Oxford University sent Kipling ten shillings with the request that he send them back "one of his finest words." He cabled back, "Thanks!"

Thanks!

Expressing appreciation is good public relations. The house organ of a large denominational overseas mission society passed on this advice: "During the holiday season many of you will receive special gifts from your supporters and friends. Please encourage those who send you gifts by sending them thank-you notes. Even though the gifts will be receipted by the Mission, your personal acknowledgment of those special gifts will greatly strengthen and encourage the long-term commitments of your churches and supporters."

There's no doubt. "Thanks" is indeed one of the finest words.

July 7 — Ordinary Blessings

A man related his miraculous escape from a burning commercial airliner in which several fellow passengers had lost their lives. A friend replied, "I have an even more remarkable experience. I have taken that very same flight, not once but a dozen times. There has never been any crash, or fire, or loss of a single life. I think I have cause for greater thanksgiving!"

A serious illness strikes. The Great Physician steps in to answer our desperate prayers. The healed man offers many thanks to the throne of mercy. Actually a greater cause for gratitude would be the many years of good health enjoyed before the sickness struck. Every day lived free of physical suffering should elicit gratitude.

Do we need a brush with death to recognize the many blessings we take for granted? We should acknowledge God's goodness in the ordinary, common, everyday course of events as well as in the unusual and dramatic affairs.

July 8 — Country of Excellent Health Care

We ought to be thankful we don't live in certain parts of the world. A missionary in one area says that when a woman is going to deliver her baby, the witch doctor takes an egg, recites mystery words, and scrubs the womb of the woman with the egg. They believe this procedure makes it easier to deliver the baby, but it often doesn't work and women die in the process.

That missionary teaches basic health education. Gradually accepting the instruction, people save money to buy mosquito nets and make safe latrines. They wash their hands before they eat, and they drink boiled water. But many tropical diseases are still prevalent. Since the people are too poor to buy medicines, the missionary provides them as much as possible. The people are thankful and begin to listen to the gospel.

How blessed we are to live in a country of excellent health care, and even more important, where the gospel of soul healing is also available.

⇒ Valley of Thanks   July 9

When Jehoshaphat, King of Judah, was attacked by the Moabites and the Ammonites with a vast army, he sought God's help. God told them to stand firm and see deliverance from the Lord. Next morning Jehoshaphat appointed men to sing to the Lord as they went out at the head of the army, saying, "Give thanks to the Lord, for his love endures forever."

As they began to sing and praise, the Lord set ambushes against the men of Ammon and Moab. The enemy was totally exterminated, leaving behind a vast array of valuable plunder, which took three days to collect.

"On the fourth day they assembled in the Valley of Beracah where they praised the Lord. This is why it is called the Valley of Beracah to this day" (2 Chron. 20:1-28). Beracah means "praise." We could call it the Valley of Thanks.

⇒ Middle C Always   July 10

A university student lived upstairs in a boarding house. Downstairs on the first floor resided an elderly, retired music teacher, then an invalid, unable to leave his apartment. Every morning the student and the retiree went through a ritual. The student would descend the steps, open the retiree's door, and ask,

"Well, what's the good news?" And the retiree would pick up his tuning fork, tap it on the side of his wheelchair, and exclaim, "That's middle C! It was middle C yesterday; it will be middle C tomorrow; it will be middle C a thousand years from now. The tenor upstairs sings flat, the piano across the hall is out of tune, but, my friend, that is middle C!" The retiree had found one thing he could depend on.

Believers can depend on the one true, immutable God whose power never abates, whose wisdom never diminishes, whose holiness never sullies, whose veracity is forever, whose love is eternal, and whose mercy is everlasting. Thank God!

≫ *July 11*   ***Can't Give That Much Money***

Years ago a man heard a sermon on tithing and promised God that he would give 10% of his income to the Lord's work. The man's weekly pay at that time was $100 a week, so he gave $10. The man rose in his company to earn $1000 a week. He gave $100 a week in tithe.

One day he asked his pastor, "How can I get released from that promise? You see—it's like this. At the beginning I had to give only ten dollars a week, but now my tithe amounts to $100 week, and I just can't afford to give away that much money."

The wise old pastor looked sadly at his parishioner. "I'm afraid I cannot get you released from your promise. But if you're not thankful to the Lord for the way He has blessed you financially, we can get down on our knees right now and ask God to shrink your income to the point where you'll again have to give only ten dollars a week!"

A better way is to thank God that we can give to his work!

≫ *July 12*   ***Count Zinzendorf***

Considered one of the greatest missionary statesmen of all times, Count Nikolaus Ludwig von Zinzendorf, born in Germany in 1700, was in many ways as influential as his better known friends, Wesley and Whitfield. He founded the Moravian movement that in its first two decades sent out more missionaries than all Protestants had sent out in the previous two centuries. He spent 33 years as supervisor of a worldwide network of overseas workers.

The event that changed the course of his life took place in his youth on a tour of Europe. In an art gallery in Dusseldorf he viewed Domenico Feti's *Ecce Homo*, a painting depicting Christ enduring the crown of thorns. Underneath was a Latin inscription, "This I have suffered for you; what have you done for me?" From that moment on Zinzendorf could never be content living the life of a nobleman. Regardless of the cost, he would follow the Savior who had suffered so much to save him.

His life became one continuous thanks.

≫ *Banishing Worry*   *July 13*

A town dweller complained to his neighbor when he bought a cock that crowed during the night. The neighbor pointed out that it crowed only three times and he didn't see how that could be an annoyance. The neighbor replied, "If you only knew what I suffer waiting for that cock to crow." Someone said that "worry is the interest we pay on trouble before it is due."

Perhaps we would get more out of our worries if we reserved certain worries for specific days of the week. Unless we worry in a logical way, we may not know where our next worry is coming from. But far better to ponder Paul's recipe for overcoming worry: "Do not be anxious about anything, but in everything, by prayer and petition, with thanksgiving, present your requests to God. And the peace of God, which transcends all understanding, will guard your hearts and your minds in Christ Jesus" (Phil. 4:6-7). We must remind ourselves of all for which we have to be thankful, and add praises to our petitions.

Thanks!

In 1737 Alexander Cruden issued his immortal work, *A Complete Concordance of the Holy Scriptures of the Old and New Testament.* Most of his life he was a bookseller and proofreader in London. However, his unbalanced mind led him to do very odd things. He called himself "Alexander the Corrector," and tried to reform the ways people kept Sunday. He carried a sponge and erased all inscriptions he considered immoral. He applied for knighthood, and even sought to marry a daughter of a lord-mayor of London.

His *Concordance* sprang from a desire to promote Bible study. In it he gives a list of nine things for which the Bible says to be thankful: spiritual blessings, moral blessings, saving grace, judgments of God on the wicked, the enlarging of Christ's kingdom, deliverance from the body of death, temporal deliverance, Christ the unspeakable gift, and deliverance of God's messengers.

He was found dead upon his knees in the act of prayer.

On a trip to South America one of the Rockefellers, to say thanks for some favor, translated "thanks a million" into Spanish by "thanks a thousand," which must have sounded a little strange coming from a Rockefeller.

Whether we say a thousand or a million thanks we infer overflowing gratitude. A constant, abounding spirit of gratitude should saturate every Christian. We should say with the Psalmist, "Every day I will praise you" (145:2). Daniel gave thanks to God three times daily (Dan. 6:10). We are told to continually offer to God a sacrifice of praise (Heb. 13:15). Paul ceased not to give thanks for the Ephesian believers (1:16). Not only are we to pray without ceasing, but we are to praise without ceasing. Being thankful shows evidence of a Spirit-filled life (Eph. 5:18-20).

Rock-bottom essence of a successful Christian life is a thankful spirit which expresses itself in grateful action.

❧ *Escape From the Taliban*   *July 16*

Heather Mercer and Dayna Curry both attended McLean Bible Church in northern Virginia. Inseparable, they decided to go to Baylor University together, then serve as humanitarian aid workers under a German relief agency in Afghanistan. There they were arrested in August 2001, along with eight other workers, on the charge of preaching Christianity to Muslims. Urgent prayers for their release were offered worldwide.

Their Hollywood-like escape after more than three months in a Taliban prison 60 miles southwest of Kabul made headlines in newspapers and TV, demonstrating big-time the power of prayer. Released by soldiers when the Taliban fled, the group was finally rescued by a U.S. Special Forces helicopter.

A night originally set for intercession for the girls' release from the Afghanistan prison turned into a celebration of thanksgiving as the girls gave their story in person. Speaking to the capacity crowd, the girls said, "It was through prayer that we were able to come out alive."

❧ *Fifteen More Years*   *July 17*

The medical report on King Hezekiah was not good. He had become seriously ill, and the prophet Isaiah's instruction was foreboding: "Put your house in order, because you are going to die; you will not recover" (Is. 38:1). Hezekiah broke down, turned his face to the wall, and wept bitterly. But God granted a reprieve. Isaiah came with another message. The Lord "will add fifteen years to your life" (38:5).

When Hezekiah recovered, he composed a song, expressing thanks and praise (38:10-20). First he conveyed his anguish on receiving his death sentence. But at the end he rejoiced, "You restored me to health and let me live. Surely it was for my benefit that I suffered such anguish . . . . you have put all my sins behind your back. The living—they praise you, as I am doing today . . . . and we will sing with stringed instruments all the days of our lives."

Many of us can thank God for recovery from sickness.

⇒ *July 18*   *Reaching a Community*

The Amy Foundation, a non-profit corporation, promotes outreach to a community by letters to editors and opinion pieces, and makes annual awards to writers of such items. One editor says that Christians should take the lead in writing letters of thanks to newspapers for all kinds of things.

He makes some suggestions. For a Cal Thomas column in the paper or a Johnny Hart cartoon. For a pot hole repair on your street, for a quality teacher in a public school. For a helpful, caring salesperson, for a city councilman who has served with dignity and class. For a coach who has been a great example for his team, for a lady who gives her time on the school board. For all kinds of things. What if these letters were simple but well crafted, containing a scriptural reference to the reason we are taking time to "give thanks with a grateful heart"? What would happen?

Well, at the very least, we would have begun. Anyone can say thanks.

⇒ *July 19*   *No Leg in the Trousers*

Someone said, "After God created the world, He made man and woman. Then to keep the whole thing from collapsing He invented humor."

On their honeymoon Nancy, the bride of Dr. Ralph Keiper, decided to press the mussed trousers of his new suit while he took a rest. Experimenting with a new iron, a wedding present, Nancy went to work. Suddenly there was a minor bang—and a puff of smoke—and a hole in his new trousers! Ralph woke up and rushed to see what had caused the bang. Nancy was in tears, worried how he would react. "Oh, honey, I was trying out our new iron and I burnt a hole in your new trousers!"

Ralph calmly replied, "Let's get down on our knees and thank God that my leg wasn't in those trousers!"

Good-natured laughter is characteristic of a strong relationship. A marriage generously sprinkled with humor isn't easily dissolved.

≫ Eyes and Ears   *July 20*

An elderly lady lay quite ill in a hospital. Her husband, now blind, was led in by a friend. After the visit he wished to kiss his wife. Leaning over the bed, he was far from her face. Seeing he needed help, the friend guided his face to her lips. Then the sound of a small smack.

Our eyes make it possible to note the outline of faces, see sunrise and sunset, distinguish between colors and movement, and read computer screens. The first astronauts, both Russian and American, exclaimed of our world from space, "What a view!"

How impoverished we would be if we had no ears. Amplified music, the sound of singing birds, the patter of gentle raindrops on the roof, the howling of the wind outside would all be lost. "Ears that hear and eyes that see—the Lord has made them both" (Prov. 20:12).

Thanks to our Creator for all our senses.

≫ Out Loud   *July 21*

A father took his two sons bowling one Saturday. Driving home, it dawned on him that neither had said, "Thank you." When he pointed this out to them, one son said, "Dad, I am thankful. I just didn't say it out loud."

David Brickner, Director of Jews for Jesus, in a recent newsletter pointed out that "something about thankfulness requires us to say it out loud. Thankfulness is not a private experience." There is a difference between being thankful and giving thanks.

Our expression of gratitude helps those around us. "Give thanks to the Lord, call on His name; make known among the nations what he has done" (1 Chron. 16:8). When individuals thankfully tell about the good things the Lord is doing in their lives, it flows over to refresh the hearts of the hearers.

If Christians thanked God more, the world would doubt Him less.

≫ *July 22*   ***Greatest Thanksgiving Text***

1 Cor. 11:25—telling how the Savior stood before His disciples less than 24 hours before He was crucified, lifted the cup, and expressed gratitude for the cup—has been called the greatest thanksgiving text in all the Bible.

That cup contained the wine which by its very color portrayed the blood He soon would shed for the sins of the world. Though this cup meant that the shadow of death was upon Him, still He could thank his Father-God.

Through Old Testament days lambs came bleating and bellowing to the brazen altar. But the true Lamb of God opened not His mouth, except to give thanks.

He knew that His blood would cleanse from all sins those who would trust in His finished work. And He thanked God. You, too, thank the Lord Jesus Christ for His death on the cross in your place. Then you can sing this chorus:

"Thank you, Lord, for saving my soul; Thank you, Lord, for making me whole;

Thank you, Lord, for giving to me Thy great salvation so rich and free."

≫ *July 23*   ***In All Circumstances***

Stuart and Jill Briscoe joined a friend whose thriving business in Northern Ireland had just been bombed by terrorists. After spending hours with other owners, raking through the smoking wreckage, this friend called everybody in the area together. He said, "Friends, this is a sad moment for us all. But it's now the early hours of the Lord's Day. So I suggest we all go home, get some sleep, and wake refreshed so that we might be found in the house of the Lord on His day. Although we have lost much, we have so much for which to thank Him, and tomorrow we should make a fresh start in acknowledging Him for all His goodness. So, let's pray together and then off you go to your beds."

They listened carefully. Many thanked him and quietly left for home. They had heard a man who gave thanks in all situations, obeying Paul's command, "Give thanks in all circumstances, for this is God's will for you" (1 Thess. 5:18).

≫ *Monica*   *July 24*

Among well-known Christian mothers is Monica, a North African Christian of the 4th century who was 23 years old when her son, Augustine, was born. He was destined to become one of the great Christian leaders of all times, despite the unbelief of his father, to whom Monica showed great respect.

Monica, who had trained Augustine in the Scriptures, must have despaired when her son went away at 16 to distant Carthage for schooling. When 18, he took up with a woman with whom he lived 13 years without marriage. She bore him a son who died at an early age. His later *Confessions* detailed his moral failures. But Augustine could not escape the memory of his mild, godly mother. Finally, at 33, he capitulated to Christ.

The historian Schaff described her reaction to the news. "She cried aloud and exulted, and her heart overflowed with thankfulness to the Lord, who, after long, long delay, had answered beyond her prayers and comprehension."

Monica's prayers were heard as well for her husband, for he too became a Christian shortly before his death.

≫ *Sentence to Solitary Confinement*   *July 25*

1500 people were congregated in a concentration camp during the Japanese occupation of China. Eggs were a treat but could only be purchased on the black market, which was run almost entirely by the Catholic Fathers, an activity they considered an act of service for the camp.

The priest at the head of the project was a mild-mannered gentleman who had scarcely spoken in 15 years because his order required the vow of silence. Now he was uncomfortable in the babble of conversation.

One day he was caught with a chicken in his hand and received his sentence—solitary confinement in a small shed. His reply was, "Thank you so much. I am used to solitary confinement and I like it."

When he began the disturbing practice of wakening at 4 a.m. and singing loud hymns of praise, it was thought wise to release him. He was soon back at his old post, thankful for solitary confinement in the same small shed again.

≫ *July 26*   *A Professor's Example of Grace*

A first-year student at Princeton Seminary enrolled in a New Testament Greek class taught by Dr. Bruce Metzger. He was fascinated with the professor's clarification of grace as undeserved forgiveness.

During a rainstorm on campus one fall Saturday morning a few weeks later, this student noticed Dr. Metzger walking nearby. Suddenly another student on a bicycle without warning ran head-on into the professor, knocking him down into a pool of water and mud. Gaining his feet, the professor tried to help the student up. Amazingly, instead of anger at the irresponsible student, Dr. Metzger apologized for getting in the boy's way and scattering his things.

Recently the first student wrote in the seminary's alumni magazine, "The years have passed since this accident, sixty of them, but hundreds of times this graduate has given thanks for the influence of his godly professor who put grace into practice."

⋙ *Each Other* — *July 27*

A young mother, an invalid, was lying on her bed half asleep when her nine-year-old daughter walked in after school. Seeing her mother without any cover over her, she unfolded the blanket at the foot of the bed and gently tucked it around her mother.

"You know," her waking mother said, "it wasn't too long ago that I was tucking you in. And now here you are tucking me in!"

The little girl bent over her drowsy mother and whispered, "We take turns," then slipped quietly out of the room.

A Christian alone in a large city wondered, if she died after work on Friday, who would miss her first, her fellow office workers on Monday, or her fellow Christians on Sunday morning. The New Testament is full of reminders to believers to love and look out for one another. In a cruel world, or in a community of believers, everybody needs somebody. Thank God for each other.

⋙ *Random Thoughts* — *July 28*

"When the Lord saves a soul, its holy joy overflows; and it cannot find channels enough for its exceeding gratitude."
—C.H.Spurgeon

"Resignation to the Divine Will signifies a cheerful approbation and thankful acceptance of everything that comes from God. It is not enough patiently to submit, but we must thankfully receive and fully approve of everything that, by the order of God's providence, happens to us. For there is no reason why we should be patient, but what is as good and as strong a reason why we should be thankful. Whenever, therefore, you find yourselves disposed to uneasiness or murmuring at anything that is the effect of God's providence over you, you must look upon yourself as denying either the wisdom or goodness of God."
—William Law (1686-1761)

≫ *July 29*   *A Chaplain's Love*

Ed Gerecke, the Lutheran Church Missouri Synod chaplain assigned to 15 war criminals on trial at Nuremberg, Germany, in late 1945, wondered if he could have any influence on Hitler's henchmen. Some rejected him. Hermann Goering, Nazi Field Marshal, resisted him to the end, though his little girl once told the chaplain that she prayed every night to "ask God to open my daddy's heart and let Jesus in."

However, Gerecke did develop a strong rapport with many. Some took communion, kneeling in their cells. At Christmas 13 of the 15 came to services. Some hummed, and a few quietly sang "Stille Nacht." In August 1946, five were sentenced to death by hanging. Gerecke accompanied them one by one to the gallows. As the rope was adjusted around the neck of Hitler's army chief Wilhelm Keitel, the two repeated a prayer. He said to the chaplain, "I thank you, and those who sent you, with all my heart."

≫ *July 30*   *The Meaning of Jesus' Grace*

The feeding of the five thousand is the only miracle recorded in all four Gospels, and all four mention Jesus saying grace.

What is involved in Jesus' grace? Sometimes the verb "give thanks" is used; sometimes the verb "bless." The content of His "grace" prayer may be gleaned from these two verbs: first, the giving of thanks, and second, the blessing. To give thanks is to gratefully recognize God as the ultimate provider of our food. To bless is to invoke divine favor on the food so it will give the eater strength and health. When Jesus prayed before feeding the five thousand, He was doing at least these two things. He thanked His heavenly Father for the provision of the loaves and fishes, and asked that this provision nourish their tired bodies. That day there was more than enough to rejuvenate the five thousand men plus women and children—12 baskets full.

We should never tire of thanking God and of asking for nourishment.

⫸ *Busy in a Good Cause* *July 31*

Just as a gauge on our car dashboard indicates the amount of gas in the tank, so our conversation reveals the level of our spiritual vitality. "If anyone is never at fault in what he says, he is a perfect man" (James 3:2).

A major reason for difficulty in governing the tongue is its wide scope for doing wrong. Some temptations provide limited opportunities for their enticements as compared to the tongue. To sin with words is a constant temptation. Speech can be violated so frequently and in so many ways, because we are using words almost incessantly. And they can so easily erupt into many aberrations such as lying, swearing, gossiping, complaining. Someone suggested the tongue is almost the last hurdle in the Christian race which, when overcome, means we have virtually arrived.

A great way to help bridle our tongue is by "always giving thanks to God the Father for everything" (Eph. 5:20).

❧ *August*

❧ *August 1*   ***When the Sun Didn't Rise***

Many things we take for granted—like the rising of the sun. A storyteller imagines a city where one day the sun didn't rise. When alarms went off, people arose in darkness, thinking it cloudy. But skies remained dark. At first, people were curious, but by 9 a.m. the phone company switchboard was swamped with calls asking if the end of the world had come.

Alarmed, people began to pray. Noon came. Then afternoon. Still dark. People went hysterical, screaming in the blackness of the street. That night few went to bed. Instead, they prayed for the sun to rise next morning. Eager eyes scanned the eastern horizon. When the first few streaks of dawn crossed the sky, soon followed by the rim of the sun, their joy knew no bounds.

The essayist Emerson said that if the stars came out only once in a century men would rush from their houses, look up into the sky, and adore. And thank!

❧ *August 2*   ***Thanks for Anesthesia***

Lucy G. Thurston, pioneer missionary to Hawaii, in a letter to her daughter in the 1850s, describes her surgery for a growing tumor of her left breast. Because of a previous paralysis she could not take chloroform. She says, "The doctor arrived. I removed my shawl, exhibiting my left arm, breast and side, perfectly bare.

"The doctor said, 'I am going to begin now.' Then came a gash long and deep, first one side of my breast, then on the other.

Deep sickness seized me . . . and deprived me of my breakfast. Friends bathed my temples devotedly . . . .

"Over an hour I was beneath his hand, in cutting out the entire breast, in tying the arteries, in absorbing the blood, in sewing up the wound, and in bandaging, and all without a drop of paregoric. Your loving mother."

Though at first so weak she had to be spoon-fed, a few months later she was back in the midst of all her duties. Thank God we now have anesthesia.

⋙ Appreciation for Life and Freedom   *August 3*

Shot down on the second day of the Gulf War, Lieutenant Colonel Acree, commander of a 320-member Marine air squadron, was soon captured, imprisoned, interrogated and beaten when he would not answer questions. A television camera caught him slumped over, head hanging toward his wrists, handcuffed, on the verge of unconsciousness and in obvious pain. He had been systematically starved and tortured.

When the war was over, he was released and soon on his way home to be reunited with his wife. She had wondered if she would ever see him again. His wife says that though he still retains scars from captivity, his experiences have left him with a deeper appreciation for life. Strolling along the Potomac, he seemed to observe the most common sights as if for the first time—a bird winging by, leaves moving in the breeze, sweet, fresh air. He would say, "Freedom is precious. You don't fully realize its value until it's taken away."

⋙ A Left-Handed Bible   *August 4*

Marek Kaminski grew up in Poland in a non-religious home. At 14 he found a Bible and came to accept its truth. He became a believer. Wanting to know more, he began to copy the Bible with his left hand, even though right-handed. He started writing when he was 19 and stopped when 22. He wrote out the first four Old Testament books, Isaiah, Psalms, the four Gospels, and Revelation, believing them very important. He is thankful for his left-handed Scripture, for by copying left-handed he had to spend much more time copying each word. He believed the attention to details by copying every word separately helped him a lot. He could tell immediately when anyone was misquoting Scripture.

Coming to the U.S. in 1984, Marek, in his mid-30s, received a doctorate in mathematics from the University of Illinois. "To me," he says, "the Bible is so beautiful. The more time you spend in it the more you appreciate it."

≫ *August 5*   *Thanks at a Tragic Time*

In April 2001, a missionary wife, Roni Bowers, 35, and her 7-month-old adopted daughter, Charity, were killed when their missionary plane was mistakenly thought to be drug-smuggling and shot down over Peru. Her husband, Jim, 37, and 6-year-old son, Cory, were also on board but neither was hurt when the pilot, Kevin Donaldson, severely wounded in both legs, managed to bring the flaming single-engine plane safely into the Amazon River.

The Bowers, serving under the Association of Baptists for World Evangelism, were river houseboat missionaries in Peru. They built their own boat, traveling the Amazon River to spread the gospel among 56 villages. The tragic shooting took place as the family was completing details on the adoption of their second child. Not long before, Roni had written, "God is in control; He knows what is best. He doesn't owe me anything. Rather, I owe Him everything."

Jim wrote, "My son, Cory, and I would like to thank [everyone for their] prayers for us at this difficult time of our lives." He also expressed forgiveness for those responsible for mistaking the missionaries for dope smugglers.

⇒⇒ *Reasons for an Offering* *August 6*

One reason Paul wrote Second Corinthians was to have the Christians there complete an offering for the relief of impoverished believers in Jerusalem. The 8th and 9th chapters are considered the classic passage on Christian giving. Paul presents motives relevant to believers of all ages.

First, giving is not throwing money away, but a generous sowing that will reap abundant returns in this life and lay up treasure above.

Second, giving will relieve the poverty of fellow-believers.

Third, generosity by his readers will evoke a chorus of praise, an "overflowing in many expressions of thanks to God" (9:12). Such a gesture would cement harmony between Jewish and Gentile believers.

Paul broke forth in a closing doxology, "Thanks be to God for his indescribable gift!" (v. 15)—certainly a reference to the Savior Jesus, the gift that makes all other gifts possible.

⇒⇒ *Giving Public Testimony* *August 7*

If you were to listen to a Billy Graham Crusade telecast, you would likely hear someone give a testimony, like Elizabeth Dole or Chuck Colson. Giving a testimony is testifying to God's goodness in one's life, often how one came to faith in Christ. Many churches have services where they invite people to give a public testimony. Reasons for thankfulness run the gamut of the Christian life. It may be praise for a negative biopsy, a successful bypass operation, or answer to prayer for a job.

When a missionary's wife was found to have inoperable cancer and later passed away, her husband testified at a church service, "We owe the Lord a deep debt of thanks for His goodness in giving us nearly 14 extra months together after her cancer was found."

Thanks!

The Psalmist said, "I will give you thanks in the great assembly; among throngs of people I will praise you" (35:18).

≫ *August 8*   ***Blessed by Losing a Job***

Arriving at the Detroit airport one afternoon, my wife arranged with a taxi driver to take her to Grosse Point. When my wife told him that her visit would be a complete surprise to her friend and all those attending her party, the driver laughed and said he wished he could see the expression on their faces.

During their conversation the taxi driver said that God had not been good to him. He had had a great job but had to quit because of the cancer threat from chemicals at work. Bernice told him about a young man attending her church, doing the same type of work. He got cancer and died. "You have been blessed by losing your job." The driver said he hadn't thought of it that way.

C.S. Lewis wrote, "We ought to give thanks for all fortune. If it is 'good,' because it is good, if 'bad' because it works in us patience, humility and the contempt of this world and the hope of our eternal country."

≫ *August 9*   ***Counting Blessings***

An itinerant Methodist preacher never failed to thank God for something, no matter how bad the situation. One Sunday he battled his way through wind and sleet to the village chapel. The small congregation wondered what he could be glad about in such weather. He prayed, "This here's a wretched day, but we thank thee that every day isn't as bad!"

David Brainerd, missionary to the Indians who died before he was 30, possessed a thankful spirit that enabled him to count his blessings in the midst of dire privations. Once when staying with friends he was suddenly taken with a toothache, a shivering cold, a high fever, and pain all over his body. Yet he thanked God that his sickness had fallen on him when he was among friends and not while alone in the wilderness.

One gloomy morning a little boy, saying grace at breakfast, thanked the Lord for "this beautiful day." To his puzzled mother he explained, "Mother, never judge a day by its weather."

≫ "My Words: What I'd Like to Do"   *August 10*

I'd like to play my piano and give piano lessons again.
I'd like to dig in the soft earth and my flower garden.
I'd like to climb a cherry tree in the summer, rake
    leaves in the fall, and make a snowman in the winter.
I'd like to knead bread, polish my silver, and clean windows.
I'd like to put on a new, long dress and pirouette all
    around the room—feeling as graceful as a ballerina.
I'd like to hold a comb, and with just a flip of the wrist
    here and there, create a new hair style every day.
I'd like to do all these things.
And I could, if I didn't have arthritis.
                    —Mildred Renfro Wade
We who can do these things—let the thanks begin!

≫ A Blind Man Who Made People See   *August 11*

Well-known author and women's conference speaker, Barbara Johnson, tells the story (source unknown) of a wife who, after a rotten day at the office, had to stand in the aisle of a late and jammed bus on the way home.

"Then I heard a deep voice up front boom, 'Beautiful day, isn't it?' Because of the crowd I couldn't see the man, but I could hear him as he called attention to scenery and various landmarks. This church. That park. This cemetery. That firehouse. Soon all the passengers were gazing out the windows. The man's enthusiasm was contagious and I found myself smiling away.

"We reached my stop. Moving toward the door, I got a look at our 'guide'. He was wearing dark glasses and carrying a thin white cane. He was blind!

"I stepped off the bus and suddenly all my built-up tensions drained away. God in His wisdom had sent a blind man to help me see—see that when all seems dark and dreary, it is still a beautiful world."

≫ *August 12*   **Sky and Mountains**

A college student, admiring the spectacular beauty of a brilliant Hawaiian sunset, yelled, "Way to go, God. Fantastic!"

A century ago eight men from England climbed the Swiss Alps Matterhorn, then yet unscaled. Four men reached the top, but four lost their footing and fell to their deaths. A survivor who had brought a prayer book along suggested they hold a funeral service and read Psalm 90, which speaks of the eternity of God who created the mountains, and of the fragility of human existence. He commented of his dear friend, "As he stood where no human had ever stood before, how thankful he must have been for that majestic panorama of sky and mountains!"

When a leader of the French revolution said to a peasant, "I will have all your church steeples pulled down so you'll not be reminded any more of your old religion," the commoner replied, "But you cannot pull down the stars!"

Thank God for sun, mountains, and stars.

≫ *August 13*   **The Influence of "Spirits"**

After attending a meeting in Williamsport, Pennsylvania, in the early 50s, I learned that my flight to Newark had been delayed by a snowstorm. Most left the airport. Only two other passengers remained. One said, "I can't think of getting on board in this weather unless I have a drink under my belt." By 9 p.m. takeoff both men were quite courageous and jovial.

We landed safely at Newark after a smooth flight. The two other passengers began to weave slowly up toward the cockpit, instead of to the side exit. I thought, "Those men are inebriated and don't know the right way out." Then I heard them express an enthusiastic thanks to the pilot for a safe trip and turn toward the exit. Under the influence of "spirits" these men did what I should have done under the control of the Holy Spirit. Wasn't there a verse, "Do not get drunk on wine . . . . Instead be filled with the Spirit . . . *always giving thanks to God the Father for everything*" (Eph. 5:18-20, italics mine).

Since then, at the end of each flight, I have tried to thank the pilots for a safe trip.

⇛ Paper, a Few Minutes, and a Stamp   *August 14*

My wife is a thank-you writer. She learned it from her high-school English teacher who, one day, said, "Instead of the usual essay assignment, I want you to hand in a different type of paper next week." She told them she had just received a thank-you from a former student that meant so much to her. "Next Tuesday hand in a thank-you letter to someone you should write."

Our daughters comment, "We hardly had time to open our Christmas presents before mother had us at the table writing thank-you notes."

A young minister prized a note from an architect: "Your sermon met me where I was on Sunday—confused and hurt. Thanks for preaching it." Those words met the pastor where he lived—discouraged and depressed—and encouraged him to keep on in the ministry. Most notes take less than 5 minutes to write and cost only a stamp, paper, and a little thought. All of us are indebted to others. Write a note in love, and walk to the mailbox this week.

⇛ Willing to Die for Another   *August 15*

In 1993 Dr. Mel Cheatham, California professor of neuro-surgery, was asked by Franklin Graham to help establish a neuro-surgery department in a 600-bed hospital for the Bosnian Muslim army in a war zone. He would be aiding Dr. Josip Jurisic, the hospital's neurosurgeon. One afternoon Dr. Cheatham operated on an Islamic guerrilla, shot through the neck. The soldier died. Next morning Dr. Jurisic said ominously, "Professor, because it was you who operated on the soldier, I fear his people will come for you and kill you." Then he said, "I have changed the medical record. I have erased your name as surgeon and written in my name in place of yours."

With a lump in his throat Dr. Cheatham said, "But surely, my friend, that means they will come for you, and they will kill you." Josip replied, "You can leave this place of war, and I cannot. I am prepared to die for you if I must."

Almost speechless with gratitude to Josip, Cheatham found himself thinking of the Great Physician who was willing to die for us on the cross.

❧ *August 16*   **Babies and Families**

At the birth of each new baby in his family, a prosperous English merchant made a special gift to some aspect of the Lord's work. Once he provided the salary for an inner-city worker; another time he paid the support of a foreign missionary. This father was saying thanks to God for each safe arrival.

Praise rose upward at the birth of babies to barren wives in the Bible. Sarah called the child of her old age "Isaac," which means laughter, for God thereby made her heart to laugh with grateful merriment. Among other mothers who rejoiced at the birth of miracle babies were Rebekah, Rachel, and Elizabeth.

Elizabeth was so overjoyed at the birth of a son (John the Baptist) late in life that she invited family and friends to rejoice with her (Luke 1:57-58).

Thank God for babies and families!

⁂ Thanks—but No Thanks   *August 17*

Sometimes there is no thanks. Or a dubious one. Or a questionable thanks. Or a genuine one.

A pastor learned from a little boy that his mother used to say a prayer for the boy at bedtime. The pastor asked what his mother prayed. He replied, "Thank God, he's in bed." That was a dubious thanks, more like a sigh of relief. Sometimes the expression, "Thank God," borders on taking God's name in vain.

A lady on relief often received grocery items from women in her church. One day she thanked a donor for a cake, then added, "But it had no icing." That was a questionable thanks, as was the suggestion of a little boy, that to save time at meals, someone offer a blanket blessing over all the groceries entering the house after each weekly shopping trip.

How refreshing one noon, when visiting a Lutheran pastor in Westchester County 15 miles north of New York City, to hear a prayer not only before, but after the meal as well. Double thanks.

⁂ He Lives   *August 18*

In 1932 Alfred H. Ackley, songwriter and pastor, was at home getting ready for the Easter Sunday morning service at his Presbyterian church in California. Flipping on the radio, he heard the speaker greet the radio audience, "Good morning—it's Easter! Folks, it really doesn't matter to me if Christ be risen or not. As far as I am concerned His body could be dust in some Palestinian tomb. The main thing is, His truth goes marching on!"

"It's a lie!" exclaimed Ackley, forgetting that the speaker couldn't hear him. "That's the whole point of Easter. He isn't dead—He's alive."

His wife said, "Why don't you write a song about it?" He took her advice, went to his piano, and out of grateful conviction wrote the gospel song, "He Lives." It begins:

"I serve a risen Savior; He's in the world today;
I know that He is living, whatever men may say."

Thanks!

August 19   ***Tender Before Tough***

Courses in Psychology 101 tell us that if we have to say something tough to a person, we should first say something tender. Commend before we correct. Paul did this in writing his letters when he had strong precepts to offer, or potent medicine to prescribe.

For example, early in his first letter to the Corinthians he wrote, "I always thank God for you because of his grace given you in Christ Jesus. For in him you have been enriched in every way" (1:4-5). He was grateful that his readers did not lag behind in any spiritual gift. Only then did he introduce several serious problems they needed to face, such as divisions in the church, blatant immorality, misunderstanding liberty, and abusing spiritual gifts.

Galatians is an exception. Paul had no thanks for them because of their serious heresy requiring circumcision for salvation. Sometimes it may be wise to omit a thanks, but often words of appreciation prepare the heart to accept truth and rebuke.

August 20   ***A Runaway Slave, His Master, and Paul***

Paul, writing to Philemon about his runaway slave Onesimus, follows his opening greeting with his usual thanksgiving and prayer, then asks a favor. Philemon's slave has come to Rome and been won to Christ by Paul, a prisoner there. The vagabond slave has become so useful to Paul that he would like to keep him there. But Paul knows that Onesimus belongs to Philemon, so Paul is returning his formerly worthless slave as a transformed brother in Christ. Paul asks Philemon to give him the same welcome he would give Paul himself.

Apparently the slave was guilty of misuse of Philemon's funds. In any case Paul promises to repay all. Philemon knows that the amount could never equal the debt that Philemon owes Paul—for he owed everything to Paul.

It's likely that Philemon welcomed Onesimus with open arms

as a Christian brother, canceled his debt, and showed him much kindness. At the end, all three—Philemon, Onesimus, and Paul—had much for which to be thankful.

⇛ *God's Inscrutable and Marvelous Ways*   *August 21*

In 1972 I flew to Hamilton, Canada, to see my father after major surgery. Next morning I found my mother on the kitchen floor, victim of a stroke. Now both parents were in the hospital— I would need help. To whom could I turn? About noon, impulsively walking downtown and stepping into a crowded store, I noticed a man, smiling in my direction. I thought the smile was meant for someone else for I lived 500 miles away. Approaching me, he asked, "Aren't you Les Flynn?" When I answered "yes," he said, "I'm Alan Marshall."

His name rang a bell. Often my parents had spoken of a highly respected lawyer in their church (where he had heard me preach). I exclaimed, "I know who you are." Mentioning my parents' situation, I said, "I may need your legal help!"

My parents both passed away within six weeks. Marshall handled their affairs most efficiently. Later he told me something remarkable. He said that he never frequented that particular store, nor did he use his noon hour to wander into any store.

How often I thank God for his inscrutable, marvelous ways.

⇛ *Good Samaritan*   *August 22*

Cleaning out old files in 2000, my wife found this note of Dec. 19, 1980: "Dear Mrs. Flynn. A Good Samaritan shoveled your path. Love, Good Samaritan." She recalled that when she first found the note those many years ago, she did some investigation and found out that the Good Samaritan was our next door neighbor boy, Joseph. His mother said that his parochial school teacher had related the story of the Good Samaritan that day and that he had decided to practice it by shoveling the snow for us, his neighbors.

Thanks!

Finding the note again in August 2000, my wife decided to return it to a grown Joseph in appreciation for a gift of love from a young boy who never told the recipient, my wife, of his kind deed. Someone coined the phrase, "random kindness." What a beautiful world it would be if we all could do something for someone else and not expect a thank-you.

☞ *August 23*   *Twosomes*

Ever notice how often Jesus used people two by two? John Broadus, in his *Commentary on the Gospel of Matthew*, shares this thought on Jesus sending out the Twelve by twos: "This arrangement may possibly have been suggested by the fact that there were among the Twelve two or three pairs of brothers, but it had also some important advantages. The two served as company for each other, preventing loneliness. They could also relieve each other in preaching to the crowds."

When Jesus sent out the Seventy, again it was by twos. He dispatched two disciples to get the colt for His "triumphant" Jerusalem entry, and two to make arrangements for the Passover in the upper room. Paul and Silas were arrested together, beaten together, sang praises together in prison. Wrote the poet, "What is the opposite of two? A lonely me, a lonely you?"

Thank God for our brothers and sisters in Christ.

☞ *August 24*   *A Child's Thank-You*

On exhibition in the George Washington Museum at Mount Vernon is a letter from G.A.G. Custis, the six-year-old adopted grandson of Martha Washington, thanking a friend for a gift.

"Dear Madam: I have received a little book which you had the goodness to send me. I wish it were in my power to make you some return for a valuable present, but I have nothing worth your acceptance but my best thanks and assurance that I will endeavor to imitate the good character, which I find described in the book. If I do this I know it will be more pleasing to you than any other return I could possibly make."

At Jesus' triumphal entry children cried to him, "Hosanna to the Son of David." When the religious leaders objected, Jesus quoted from the Psalms, "From the lips of children and infants you have ordained praise" (Matt. 21:15-16).

If little children thank, how much more should mature adults?

≫ Angelic Praise   *August 25*

Angels sang together at creation. David asked the angels to join in a great psalm of praise (Ps. 103:20-21). The angelic host praised God at the birth of Christ. Glimpses into heaven indicate that thankful praise is one of the functions of celestial beings. The four living creatures, likely cherubim, "give glory and honor and thanks to him who sits on the throne and who lives for ever" (Rev. 4:9).

Another view reveals all the angels standing before the throne and around the elders and the four living creatures. They fall on their faces before the throne, saying: "Amen! Praise and glory and wisdom and thanks and honor and power and strength be to our God for ever and ever. Amen!" (Rev. 7:11-12).

If in heaven thanks is rendered the Almighty by his angelic creatures, should not likewise thanks be given him now by his redeemed human family on earth?

≫ Some Musings   *August 26*

A godly woman in her nineties was feeling her age in every joint and bone. "Old age ain't for sissies!" she groaned audibly. Then, as always, her groans gave way to praise for God's goodness. A focus on gratitude, begun early in life, parted the clouds and let the sun shine in.

A veteran missionary received sad news from home. Though

he prayed, the darkness deepened. Then on a visit to a mission home he saw on the wall these words: TRY THANKSGIVING. Before long the shadow was gone. The Psalmist is right: "It is good to give thanks to the Lord."

An anonymous poem, entitled, *My Fourfold Prayer*, gives thanks to God:

For the gift of strength and health
And for friendship's boundless wealth,
For the power to think aright,
And for the Bible's guiding light—
We give Thee thanks.
Gratitude is the memory of the heart.
—Jean-Baptiste Massieu

≫ *August 27*   ***Grateful Better than Gripeful***

A mother in Canada, who had lived in England during World War II, was unhappy to hear her teenage daughter complain about the meals served at home. She went to the library to check on what food she as a girl had eaten during the London blitz. Then she put her daughter on the same diet: a week's ration of 14 ounces of meat, 3 eggs, 2 pounds of potatoes, and 2 ounces of cheese. For Sunday dinner the teenager was served bread and butter and a hard-boiled egg. Said the daughter, "I'll never complain again."

Jesus never complained. Rather he was known for His grateful spirit. In fact, one of the ways He was recognized was by the thankful way He presided at meals. On the afternoon of His resurrection He joined two disciples on the road to Emmaus who ironically failed to recognize Him during a long conversation along the way. It was not until He sat down in their home to eat that recognition broke through. As He blessed the bread and broke it, it was then "they recognized him" (Luke 24:31).

How much better to cultivate an appreciative outlook than a complaining disposition.

⇒ *On the Tip of Our Tongue*   *August 28*

Our thoughts, if unchecked, rise up into words and deeds. If we could learn to be slow to speak (James 1:19), we would slow down any angry thoughts we might be entertaining. It would give time for the potentially boiling passion within to slowly abate and never reach the level of explosive speech or deeds.

Experience teaches us that often when something is on the tip of our tongue we should have kept it there. Someone quipped, "Look before you lip." Often we conquer our unwise passions by refusing to let them be expressed in words. Bonhoeffer termed this "the ministry of holding one's tongue."

In our slowness to speak, recall some reason for gratitude. Think thanks. An excellent extinguisher of potential flames is a flow of thankful words.

"An attitude of gratitude can make your life a beatitude."

⇒ *Diary of Recovery*   *August 29*

A traveling business executive who lived at top speed was flattened to his back by a severe heart attack, becoming an invalid unable to tie his shoe laces. With no visitors allowed he turned to new friends—animals, birds, and flowers. His diary of recovery vibrates awareness of discovery—discovery of a world previously accepted so casually, and often unexamined.

Having to learn all over again to stand, to walk, to use arms and hands, and even to put food in his mouth, he recognized afresh the simple blessings of health, and expressed great gratitude. The coming of spring seemed to say, "There is a God. And there is life beyond the grave." He confessed, "My world had been a thousand friends in a hundred cities, ten cups of coffee, and loud talk till three in the morning. Now my world is reduced to my home, my farm, my hills. I live more closely with my wife, my daughter, my animal friends. I think more deeply of God."

And, of course, he thanked more.

Thanks!

» *August 30*   ***A Grateful Heart***

When Chuck Colson was released from prison, his wife Patty had to adjust to his new perspectives. He would just walk around the house and suddenly yell out, "Patty, come look at this beautiful sky." He would get excited about roses in the yard and everything else.

A practice of St. Ignatius, at the end of the day, was not only to examine his conscience by meditating on his sins, but also to meditate on the good things that had happened.

George Herbert (1593-1633) penned this thanksgiving prayer: "Thou Who has given so much to me, give one more thing—a grateful heart, not thankful when it pleases me, (as if Thy blessings had spare days,) but such an heart whose pulse may be Thy praise."

Luci Shaw prayed, "Make of our hearts a field to RAISE your PRAISE."

How good to say with the Psalmist, "I go about your altar, O Lord, proclaiming aloud your praise (26:6-7).

» *August 31*   ***Thanks for Individual Freedoms***

Recently the World Evangelical Fellowship (WEF) Religious Liberty Commission coordinated a program of the International Prayer for the Persecuted Church in 130 different countries, spotlighting the little known but widespread plight of suffering believers in so many parts of the world. How thankful we should be for our freedoms.

Well I recall how soon after a Sunday morning service in Europe a few years ago, a woman who had been present and had gone home came running back to the pastor, breathless and terrified. Her husband had just been arrested and was in prison, where he could be held six months without a charge.

No wonder that Paul urged, "then, first of all, that requests, prayers, intercession and thanksgiving be made for everyone— for kings and all those in authority, that we may live peaceful and quiet lives in all godliness and holiness" (1 Tim. 2:1-2).

❧ September

❧ *A Throne That Cannot Be Shaken* · *September 1*

Kings of this earth, once enthroned, are now dethroned. Dynasties disappear. But there's one throne that will never crumble. The throne of God will never fall because it cannot be shaken.

Persecuted Hebrew Christians received this message: "Since we are receiving a kingdom that cannot be shaken, let us be thankful, and so worship God acceptably with reverence and awe" (Heb. 12:28).

Hong Kong recently changed from its status as a British colony to Chinese sovereignty. Shortly before the British flags were lowered in the ceremonies at the Hong Kong East Tamar parade ground, the marching bands played a quiet hymn. Written in 1878 by John Ellerton, the last stanza reads,

> So be it Lord; Thy throne shall never,
> Like earth's proud empires, pass away;
> Thy kingdom stands, and grows forever,
> Till all thy creatures own Thy sway.

Thank God for His everlasting throne.

❧ *His Eye Is on the Sparrow* · *September 2*

Civilia D. Martin, wife of an evangelist, wrote the hymn, "God Will Take Care of You." Visiting a bedridden invalid in Elmira, New York, Mrs. Martin asked if she didn't sometimes get discouraged. The invalid replied, "How can I be discouraged when my Heavenly Father watches over each little sparrow, and I know He loves and cares for me? I'm so thankful!"

Mrs. Martin procured paper and pencil, and in a few minutes had written the words to "His Eye Is on the Sparrow." Someone mailed the words to songleader Charles M. Alexander. The song was first sung in London's Royal Albert Hall during the Torrey-Alexander revival in 1905. From there these words from a thankful, trusting invalid have gone everywhere:

> Why should I feel discouraged, Why should the shadows come,
> Why should my heart be lonely And long for Heav'n and home,
> When Jesus is my portion? My constant Friend is He:
> His eye is on the sparrow, And I know He watches me.

≫ *September 3*   ***Safe in the Arms of Jesus***

The Salvation Army magazine, *The War Cry*, told the story of seven Russian soldiers, captured by the Finnish army in World War II, who were to be shot at dawn. The atmosphere was filled with hatred. The guards taunted the prisoners who swore and beat the walls. Suddenly, a doomed man began to sing, "Safe in the arms of Jesus, Sweetly my soul shall rest." All thought him mad.

The singer quietly said, "It's from the Salvation Army. I heard it three weeks ago. At first I also laughed at this song, but it reminded me of the crucified Savior. Soon I thanked Jesus, and since then this verse has been sounding inside me. In a few hours I shall be with the Lord." His face shone. Then some prisoners began to beg God for mercy. All began to sing. Guards joined in. Other hymns long since forgotten came forth from their memories.

The clock struck six. Between two rows of guards they marched out to face execution. They asked permission to sing once more. When the last lines died out, came the command, "Fire!" The seven Red soldiers went singing into heaven.

⋙ *Who Really Owns Them?* *September 4*

A day after her grandmother's funeral, a little girl noticed that her mother brought home a pair of brass candlesticks from grandmother's mantel. The girl asked, "Mother, do you own them now that grandmother is gone?"

Mother replied, "Nearly a hundred years ago great-grandfather purchased them. He thought he owned them because he paid for them. But after a while he died and Aunt Sue kept them for many years. Then they came to your grandmother. Now grandma is gone, and the candlesticks have come to me. Who really owns them?" She paused a moment, then continued. "Each one may have possessed them for a few years, but none really owned them. The Lord is the real owner."

Our offering to the Lord, perhaps in a special way our tithe, is our acknowledgment of God's ownership of all our possessions—a sort of rent on his property. Recognizing the range of our assets will help us to "give thanks to the Lord of lords" (Ps.136:3).

⋙ *The Three "G's"* *September 5*

The biography of every Christian can be summed up in three words—the three "G's": guilt, grace, gratitude.

Guilt. God is a holy God, and entrance into heaven requires perfection in his creatures. But "all have sinned" and fall short of God's standard (Rom. 3:23). We are all guilty before God.

Grace. On the cross Jesus suffered the penalty of our sins, taking on Himself our guilt. If we accept Him as our Savior, we receive the forgiveness of sin and become the children of God, all totally unmerited.

Gratitude. The essence of salvation is a genuine, life-revolutionizing thankfulness for the cross and empty tomb of Jesus Christ. The master key of thankfulness unlocks the door not only to salvation, but also to worship, generosity, contentment, morality, and dedication. The Christian life is really one continuous "Thank you, Jesus."

※ *September 6*   **Thanks in Bereavement**

Nine months after the death of Harland Hastings, a Nova Scotian and a member of the Board of Directors of the Billy Graham Association of Canada, his wife, Jennifer, wrote that nothing had prepared her for the loneliness, hurt, loss, and emptiness that she would experience. She now had to live day-by-day without her husband, lover, friend, and dearest companion with whom she had prayed, laughed and cried for nearly 50 years.

Though receiving strong support from family and friends, she wrote, "Closure was something that I would have to go through alone. Longing for a human presence not there, I began to understand that someone was there. Despite my hurt God was always present. I began to practice what I had been taught to do. The Bible says, 'give thanks in all circumstances, for this is God's will for you in Christ Jesus' (1 Thes. 5:18). I started by giving thanks to God for loaning me a true Christian gentleman, who had been the human head of our home and family. I press on, knowing that God is in control."

※ *September 7*   *Always Something to Be Thankful For*

A Connecticut congregation had fallen into the habit of coming late to church. The new pastor's grateful spirit helped remedy the situation. His invocation one Sunday morning first thanked the Lord for those present. He then expressed thanks for those passing up the aisles, next for those lingering about the door, or coming up the church steps. Then he uttered gratitude for those getting out of their cars, for those on the highway, for those just leaving their homes. Finally, he thankfully closed his petition for those reaching the door in time for the benediction.

An elderly couple that had visited their son 15 consecutive

Christmases were disappointed when ill health prevented the 500-mile trip the next December. Instead of complaining, they thanked God for the wonderful 15 Christmases they had had together.

Swedish proverb: "Those who wish to sing always find a song."

⋙ *Cure for Pessimism* *September 8*

The novelist Chesterton tells the story of a young Oxford tutor who complained of the dreary view of a silly duck pond from his second-floor rooming house. In his lectures he often commented on the futility of existence, concluding that the only sane action would be to end it all.

A well-built student decided to test the tutor. He knocked on his door and brandished a revolver, declaring he had come to put the tutor out of his meaningless existence. The terrified tutor, suddenly losing his philosophy and begging for his life, climbed out his window onto a flagpole, hoping to attract some passerby. The student, sitting on the windowsill and waving his revolver, forced the tutor, perched precariously on the flagpole, to give thanks for his unhappy life, even for the ducks in the pond. In full surrender the weary tutor climbed back to freedom, promising to do less complaining.

Robinson Crusoe said, "All our discontents spring from the want of thankfulness for what we have."

⋙ *Acknowledgment of Divine Protection* *September 9*

Ezra, the priest, requested permission of Artaxerxes, King of Persia, to go up to Jerusalem to investigate the condition of an earlier band of exiles who had returned to Jerusalem. Artaxerxes not only granted this request, but also gave a large gift of money from the royal treasury to help out.

Their travel route invited attacks by thieves. If Ezra asked for military protection, it might seem that his God wasn't a very strong God. Ezra decided to show faith, and he noted gratefully that God's hand granted them safe arrival with their valuable cargo still intact (Ezra 8:31).

The Book of Common Prayer has a prayer entitled, "For A Safe Return from a Journey." It's for a traveler who has safely passed through the perils of the great deep "who now desireth to return his thanks unto thee in thy holy Church. May he . . . ever express his thankfulness by a holy trust in thee, and obedience to thy laws, through Jesus Christ our Lord. Amen."

≫ *September 10*   *An Archbishop of Canterbury*

In a day when toleration seems to compromise virtue, how refreshing to read these words of the former Archbishop of Canterbury, George Carey, in *The Anglican Digest*. Reflecting on his many meetings with other religions over his nine years as Archbishop, he says, "I have been led to embrace two overlapping ideas. First, that a high Christology does not mean intolerance and fanaticism.

"Second, that it is possible to be a wholehearted Christian and still be able to understand, accept, and work with persons of other faith traditions . . . . I have said to people of other faiths that my faith is so important to me that I am compelled to share it and to offer it to you as a gift. But in inviting you to partake of this gift, I too must have the humility to listen to your story of believing. However . . . . All religions are not the same, and Jesus Christ is not merely one great religious figure among others. Rather, he is unique, incomparable and the gift to be shared."

In other words, the Archbishop is saying, if we interpret him accurately, that he is willing to listen to others share their religions, but that the gift he is sharing, and inviting them to receive, is Jesus Christ, incomparable and unique, the only way.

≫ Escaping the Twin Towers on 9/11   *September 11*

I shall never forget the Sunday following the 9/11 terrorist attack on the World Trade Towers, 30 miles from our church. A member of our church, Mark Beukema, who had worked among refugees for two decades in the Far East, then with United Seaman's Service, was in his office that morning on the 21st floor of Building #1. He said, "I felt the building shake and heard alarms go off and warnings to get out. I grabbed my briefcase. The office secretaries followed. We walked down 21 flights and were soaked at the ground from the sprinklers. Bodies and debris were all around. Covered with ash, and groping in the blinding, black smoke, we found ourselves at the edge of the Hudson River. A fireboat suddenly appeared. We jumped on board. With about a hundred others we were whisked to Jersey City and safety."

Two other men from our congregation who had also escaped that morning joined Mark in excited conversation after the service. We all rejoiced with great thanksgiving for all who escaped, and mourned the loss of those who had perished.

≫ Respect and Appreciation   *September 12*

A noted papyrologist at the University of Michigan was often asked by his fellow scholars in the department to call the janitor to come when something went wrong in their office. One day he asked his fellow workers, "Why do you always ask me to get the janitor?"

They answered, almost in chorus, "Because he will come sooner when you request it."

He looked at them. "Do you know why?"

When they answered they didn't have a clue, the papyrologist gave a jarring explanation. "It's because you never show him any appreciation. Do you know his full name? Do you know anything about him? The janitor and the other workers keep this place going. Without them we would be lost. It's about time you thanked them and realized how much you owe them."

Paul wrote to the Romans, "Give everyone what you owe him: . . . if respect, then respect; if honor, then honor" (Rom. 13:7-8).

≫ *September 13*   *Search for a Nail*

Bob Pierce, founder of World Vision, told of a missionary who, moving into a village of Stone Age people in Sumatra's dense jungles, lost no time in telling them the gospel. They interrupted the interpreter several times. "What is a cross?" they asked.

Cutting down a tree, the missionary formed a cross on the ground and stretched himself on it. They wanted to know what a nail was—they had never seen one. The missionary searched high and low for something that resembled a nail, but found nothing. Later, handling a can of fruit, he heard a rattle. Looking inside, he saw a nail at the bottom.

"Thank you, Lord," he shouted. He rushed to the chief who quickly gathered the villagers. Then he explained how the point of a large nail was pounded into Christ's hands. Many accepted Christ.

The chief, nail in hand, often helped the missionary on tour explain the gospel.

≫ *September 14*   *Enduring Our Blessings*

A bachelor who earned a degree in child rearing gave lectures on "Ten Commandments for Raising Children." After marriage and the birth of his first child, he changed the title to "Five Commandments for Raising Children." When his second child arrived, the title became "Some Suggestions for Raising Children." After his third child arrived, he quit lecturing. But despite the problems along the way, he found many joys and learned many lessons.

Even when children get older and sometimes unruly, parents would rather have them noisy than sick. One Thanksgiving dinner a mother spoke to her guests about her blessings, mentioning her four healthy children. Later when pandemonium reigned in the house, a friend noticed the mother with eyes closed. The mother explained, "I'm just praying for patience to endure my blessings."

When a child achieves character and success in later years, wise parents say, "We're proud of our child." Even better, "We're thankful."

⇘ *South Pacific Christians*   *September 15*

Jesus warned against thinking that familiarity with His name proves divine acceptance. "Not everyone who says to me, 'Lord, Lord,' will enter the kingdom of heaven, but only he who does the will of my Father who is in heaven" (Matt. 7:21).

A book entitled *They Found the Church There* told of World War II servicemen marooned on South Pacific islands. They were befriended by natives, who hid them, fed them, and even quoted Bible verses to them. These natives had become Christians through missionaries who had previously come to the island. Though the U.S. servicemen had been born in America where the gospel is widely proclaimed in churches and over radio and TV, many had missed the gospel message. But now their "heathen" rescuers taught the gospel to civilized U.S. servicemen and led many to Christ.

Some employees in a Christian publishing company were not believers though they packed up thousands of books that explained the way to heaven.

We should beware of taking for granted what we ought to take with gratitude.

⇘ *Salvation in All Its Phases*   *September 16*

In his second letter to the Thessalonians, Paul writes, "But we ought always to thank God for you, brothers loved by the Lord, because from the beginning God chose you to be saved through the sanctifying work of the Spirit and through belief in the truth. He called you to this through our gospel, that you might share in the glory of our Lord Jesus Christ" (2 Thes. 2:13-14).

Paul declares his gratitude "because from the beginning God chose you to be saved." This is known as the doctrine of election and honors the sovereignty of God. The believer works out this salvation through the sanctifying power of the Holy Spirit, trans-forming moral character. The end of this call is future "sharing in the glory of our Lord Jesus Christ."

Charles R. Erdman says, as Paul "attributes this salvation to the divine choice, wrought out by divine power, made effective through a divine message, and perfected in divine glory, it is inevitable that he should give thanks to God."

⋙ *September 17*   *Miracles at an Orphanage*

In the 1830s, with only two shillings in his pocket, George Muller started an orphanage in Bristol, England which cared for 10,000 orphans over a 60-year period. He operated the orphan-age without making known any need, all by faith and prayer.

Never did the children go without a meal. One morning when not a speck of food or milk was on hand to feed the hun-dreds of hungry orphans, Muller prayed, "Father, we thank Thee for the food Thou art going to give us." Came a knock at the door. A baker stood there. "I was awakened at 2 a.m. and felt I should bake some bread for you." A few minutes later came another knock. A milkman said, "My milk wagon just broke down in front of your place. I must get rid of these cans of milk before I can take the wagon for repairs. Can you use this milk?" Muller testified that incidents like this happened hundreds of times.

At the grave of Lazarus, before raising him from the dead, Jesus prayed, "Father, I thank you that you have heard me," then called Lazarus forth.

≫ *Guardian Angels* *September 18*

Dr. Clyde Taylor, founder of the National Association of Evangelicals, told me this story one night when we were hotel roommates at a World Relief Committee meeting. As a young missionary in Peru he paid a courtesy call on the local chief to explain why he had come to the area. Later, at dusk, spotting a big canoe holding several men, and hearing whistling which he knew were signals, Taylor sensed something wrong. He and his friends decided to stay out in the jungle that night. Two years later that chief became a believer, admitting, "We intended to kill you that night. But you were too many. On your roof were crowds of men, all in white robes."

The Psalmist says, "The angel of the Lord encamps around those who fear him, and he delivers them" (34:7). Elijah saw angels form a circle of protection around Dothan. Angels rescued Daniel from the lions and unchained Peter and opened his prison gate. How thankful we are that they guard us in all our ways (Ps. 91:11).

Yes, God's children are often "touched by an angel."

≫ *In a Chaplain's Pocket* *September 19*

The wife of a U.S. Army chaplain found ironing her husband's uniform a chore, so she was delighted to find a laundry which would starch and crease it for $1.50. They picked up and delivered every Monday. No one at the house seemed to remember to empty the pockets. Pens and hankies went into the laundry's trash bin. Also discarded were the chaplain's many lists, and even his prayers.

One Monday morning Betty, the delivery girl, arrived at the door, not with her usual sullen look, but glowing. "I want to thank you for the prayers. Every week I clean out the pockets of your husband's fatigues. I thought that God had given up on me, but he has been speaking to me through the prayers I found in your husband's pockets." She told of her past traumas: abuse, abortion, divorce. "Those scraps of papers with prayers were like food. I couldn't wait till Monday to see if I would find another prayer with its message. Yesterday I accepted Jesus as my Savior, and my new church has a group that cares for me."

≫ *September 20*   *Let's Roll*

It was on September 20, 2001, that President Bush at a joint session of Congress gave special recognition and thanks to Lisa Beamer, widow of Todd Beamer who died on United Airlines Flight #93 after joining an heroic effort to wrest the aircraft from hijackers. The fourth plane commandeered that morning crashed in the Pennsylvania countryside, averting another disaster like the Twin Towers and the Pentagon, possibly the White House.

In the last minutes of the doomed flight Todd Beamer spoke on an Airfone with a supervisor, telling of the passengers' plan to overpower the hijackers. He asked her to pray with him. The last words she heard him say were, "Are you guys ready? Let's roll." Then screams and a scuffle before the line went dead.

Lisa Beamer testified publicly, "God's controlled the whole situation, and though it may not make much sense now, I know that someday it will all make sense. It already makes sense when people tell me Todd gave his life to help others."

≫ *September 21*   *Every Careless Word*

A group of husbands were laughing in the living room after a dinner party. When the ladies joined the men in the living room, the host announced, "I've had my new recorder on while you were in the kitchen. I thought you might like to hear what the men were saying."

Immediately one man who had told an off-color story turned red. The recorder was switched on. Out came the conversation word for word. As it neared the joke, the storyteller began to squirm in his chair. Then out came his voice. It was about to reach the dirty punch line. Suddenly the doorbell rang. Several exclaimed loudly, "There's someone at the door!" drowning out the end of his story. The man gave a sigh of relief, smiled, then wiped the perspiration from his forehead.

Thank God we can have the penalty of our careless words blotted out by the forgiveness of Christ. But unless we face up to our speech now, we will have to account for "every careless word" in the day of judgment (Matt. 12:36).

⫸ Out of God's Sight, Memory, and Reach   *September 22*

People try to get rid of their sins in various ways. They neutralize, rationalize, minimize, revise, or anesthetize them, but discover that the one that hides his sin does not prosper. Rather, "Blessed is he whose transgressions are forgiven, whose sins are covered" (Psalm 32:1). Then our sins are:

Out of God's sight. King Hezekiah wrote, "you have put all my sins behind your back" (Is. 38:17). And God won't turn around to look at them.

Out of God's memory. God says, "I will . . . remember their sins no more" (Jer. 31:34)—expunged, never to be held against us again.

Out of God's reach. "As far as the east is from the west, so far has he removed our transgressions from us" (Ps.103:12). But east is east and west is west, and never the twain shall meet. One lady said that when Satan reminded her of her sins, she just kept sending him back and forth between the east and the west.

What a great reason to be thankful—our sins are out of God's sight, memory, and reach!

⫸ A Quiet Time   *September 23*

A young couple, recognizing the need for a quiet time of prayer and thanksgiving, tried an experiment. In the evening,

Thanks!

one watched the youngsters while the other went into the bed-
room to pray. After a half-hour they changed places. The plan
never worked. The wife would hear the squeak of a linen closet
door opening in the hallway outside. Knowing that her toddler
could empty the lower shelves, she kept hoping for someone to
close it. Then the phone would ring. She thought, "Someone
answer, please." Before she knew it, the half-hour was up.

One day a neighbor told about his new job at the airport.
"The noise of those jets is unbelievable. I wear ear protectors like
a headset." The wife thought, "Headset?" A few evenings later she
adjusted a pair of stereo headphones for silence. The change was
remarkable. She couldn't hear a thing. "Lord, I thank you," she
prayed. "Now I can tune you in."

⇒ *September 24*   **AARP Praises**

Esther "Tess" Canja, president of AARP (American
Association of Retired People) heaped praise on a 20-year-old
Western Union teller whose quick thinking outwitted crooks
from taking a substantial portion of the life savings of an elderly
Stockton, California, man. Noticing how nervous the man
seemed, the suspicious clerk discovered that the intended victim
had been told by phone that he had won a Canadian lottery, but
to claim his prize he had to send the caller thousands of dollars to
cover taxes.

Western Union clerk Marisol Alcazar called the police about
a possible scam. The crooks were apprehended, and the man
eventually got his money back, plus some other money he had
previously sent to other scam operators.

When Esther "Tess" Canja learned how Alcazar's quick thinking outwitted the crooks, she wrote her a letter, "On behalf of
AARP, thank you for being alert and caring, and may the good
that you do come back a hundredfold."

⇛ Leftovers   *September 25*

For thirteen years a clergy couple handled the "Since You Asked" column in *The Lutheran*, a monthly magazine of the Evangelical Lutheran Church. In their final column, they cited a favorite question asked through the years, probably with tongue in cheek, "Do we have to pray over leftovers?"

Their response: "No, we get to pray over leftovers. We are thankful we have leftovers and mindful of the needs of those who have no food at all."

If the leftovers constitute a main meal, and grace is a habit at mealtime, prayer is likely said. However, prayer is probably optional at coffee break, afternoon tea, a late night snack, or evening socializing. Regardless of whether or not we offer thanks for anything other than our main meals, what is important is that in our hearts we subscribe to a continuous, deep-down thanksgiving to Almighty God for His provisions.

A prayer in *The Book of Common Prayer* is titled, "Thanksgiving to Almighty God for the fruits of the earth and all the other blessings of his merciful providence."

⇛ Praying Hands   *September 26*

Albrecht Durer, wishing to draw and paint, left home to study. He shared a room with an older man with the same goal. Both barely existing, the friend insisted on working while Durer continued to study, and when Durer was successful they would trade roles. So, the friend worked long hours scrubbing floors, anticipating his turn at using his brush again. At last the day came when Durer sold a woodcarving at a price sufficient to cover expenses for a long time. "Now, it's your turn," Durer said to his old friend.

So his old friend took up his brush. But stiffened muscles, enlarged joints, and twisted fingers had destroyed his artistic ability. One day Durer returned to find his friend praying with his work-worn hands reverently folded. He thought, "I can never give him back the lost skill of those hands, but I can show the world my gratitude for his noble deed. I'll paint his gnarled hands as they now are folded." Durer's "Praying Hands" is a reminder of that appreciation.

≫ *September 27*   **Restored Abilities**

Armless and legless, a courageous soldier left Walter Reed Hospital with a wave. A hand grenade had caused his mishap four years before. Doctors supplied him with artificial limbs. The 25-year-old youth, a carpenter before his accident, had discovered he could once again nail down a board. His face lit up as he said, "My gratefulness knows no bounds."

At a Thanksgiving dinner in New York City, a mother said, "The holiday will take on added meaning because my three-year-old son will give me a morning kiss, something he has just learned to do." A victim of cerebral palsy from birth, with no muscular control, the boy had been learning to control arms, legs, facial muscles, and back. Able to sit up, crawl, move about in a walker, help feed and wash himself, he had just been taught to master a few words: "no," "mama," "daddy." When taught to purse his lips to form the letters, he also learned to kiss. More reason for thanks.

≫ *September 28*   **Hearing and Sight**

Think of some everyday things we give little thought to: waking up each morning, going to sleep, talking, walking, eating, swallowing, reading, remembering, laughing, breathing, tasting, feeling, seeing, and hearing. Let's not take them for granted.

I recall suddenly losing much of my hearing in 1990 after flying on two successive weekends while on medication for a sinus infection. I developed difficulty catching a conversation when in a small group. On my return my ear doctor put a tube in each ear, the procedure taking only a few minutes. Suddenly the silence was broken—I could hear the traffic rushing by outside his office. I experienced a morsel of the exultation of the deaf man Jesus healed.

In 1993, unable to see the big E on the chart with my left eye, I was considered legally blind in that eye. My ophthalmologist, concerned, removed the cataract. Immediately I could see clearly. Later I had surgery for a cataract on my other eye. Again, I felt a tiny measure of the thrill and gratitude of blind people healed by Jesus.

⇛ *The Church Forever*   *September 29*

An exhibit in a world's fair a few years back was billed as "The City of Tomorrow." This miniature model projected the concept of several sociologists. It had moving sidewalks, double-decker streets, and variously shaped glass structures. The city had no churches. A sociologist said, "Our studies indicate no churches will be needed in the city of tomorrow."

The sociologist must have been unaware of Jesus' promise, "I will build my church, and the gates of Hades will not overcome it" (Matt. 16:18). Not long ago workmen, repairing the great mosque in Damascus, found these words graven over the front door: "Thy kingdom, O Christ, is an everlasting kingdom." Though originally a Christian church, for over 1200 years it has been ranked among the holiest sanctuaries of the Muhammadan faith. Yet strangely the Christian inscription has remained in its place as if to prove that no power can destroy the everlasting church. Hallelujah!

⇛ *Easter and the Offering Plate*   *September 30*

The great resurrection chapter in the New Testament is 1 Corinthians 15. Paul begins by declaring that Christ "was raised on the third day," and ends by assuring believers of a resurrection with perfect bodies. He writes, "Thanks be to God!" and urges steadfastness.

Then Paul swings from the excitement of the resurrection into the topic of money. The next four words read, "Now about the collection" (1 Cor. 16:1). Though these words are in the next chapter, remember there is no chapter break in Paul's original writing. Paul speaks of resurrection victory and church offerings in the same breath. The gospel and money are closely related.

Paul mentions an offering to be received "on the first day of the week." How logical to give an offering on the first day, for Sunday is the day that commemorates the resurrection of Jesus from the grave. Out of gratitude for His victory over death we should not only gather to worship Him, but also gladly bring a gift on the weekly anniversary of this triumphant event.

❧ October

❧ Countless Blessings

October 1

MaryEv Ketcham was visiting her husband, "Deak" Ketcham, vice-president of Gordon College, who was seriously ill in New England Baptist Hospital in Boston. She stopped to visit the woman in the next room and noticed how despondent she was. The lady had just had a spinal fusion. MaryEv gently suggested that she count her blessings. A few days later MaryEv visited her again and found her happy. The woman pointed to a tall white building out the window, "See—it has 122 windows. I have counted a blessing for every window."

A week before she died at age 101, under three strong medicines, Mabel Canberg had some lucid moments of reflection on a long life of goodness and practical Christianity. She began telling her daughter, Mary, a list of all the things for which she was thankful. Using the alphabet, she began with the letter "a." Said Mary, "She gave thanks really for everything. She knew the end was coming, and she was thankful for her whole life."

❧ Wilderness Wanderings

October 2

Coming downstairs one morning, an English peer heard the cook grumble, "Oh, if only I had five pounds, wouldn't I be content!" Shortly after, the nobleman handed her a five-pound note. She thanked him profusely. Leaving the room he heard her say, "Why didn't I say ten?" Her story is reminiscent of the Israelites' wilderness wanderings.

Thanks!

The Israelites had barely crossed the Red Sea—miraculously—and escaped Egypt when they began griping about water too bitter to drink (Ex. 15:23-24). This was the first in a long series of complaints recorded during the wilderness wanderings. The book of Numbers could well be called the book of Murmurings or Thanklessness. Had not their memories been so short they would have been thanking God for His providence instead of grumbling about their privations. God commands us to "forget not all his benefits" (Ps. 103:2).

Memories of thankfulness always prevent discontent.

≫ *October 3*   **Our Blessing Bag**

Karen worried a lot. She had just divorced. Her eldest daughter had gone overseas. Her son was living in his car. Her youngest daughter was living with her dad, and seemed distant. And her new marriage to a man she loved was suffering financial insecurity. She focused on her problems.

A friend advised, "You can't continue worrying so much. Write down your blessings on slips of paper and put them in a little bag, a few every day. Sometime look at what you wrote. The things that bug you now will begin to fade."

Karen found a small gift bag and wrote on it, "Our Blessing Bag." She and her husband began recording their blessings that January day. The bag began to overflow. On Thanksgiving morning they turned the bag upside down. They took turns reading blessings, all but forgotten: a trip, Christian son-in-law, a quick recovery from a leg injury, a new job, and so on.

Says Karen, "We still give thanks daily. Gratitude is our middle name."

≫ *October 4*   **Daily Practice**

Vaughn Shoemaker, for many years cartoonist for the *Chicago Daily News* and twice Pulitzer Prize winner, went to his knees every morning before starting work. He would not create a cartoon without first thanking God for his God-given talent and asking God to guide his hand as he began to draw.

Though prayer had always been significant to the late Kenneth Taylor, publisher of *The Living Bible*, it was in seminary when prayer and daily devotional Bible reading became important. Someone told him the value of writing down on an index card the items to be remembered in prayer, then checking them off when the answers came. He said it was a great joy to be able to cross off the answered petitions. But he had long since found an advanced step that enhanced his prayer life considerably. He said, "Instead of immediately crossing off the answered item, I put a check mark beside it, and for several days . . . give thanks before going on to other items."

A Pharisee and a Tax Collector   *October 5*

A person may seem to be thanking God when in fact he's really only congratulating himself. Jesus spoke of two men who "went up to the temple to pray, one a Pharisee and the other a tax collector. The Pharisee stood up and prayed about himself: 'God, I thank you that I am not like all other men . . . or even like this tax collector. I fast twice a week and give a tenth of all I get.' But the tax collector stood at a distance. He would not even look up to heaven, but beat his breast and said, 'God, have mercy on me, a sinner'" (Luke 18:9-13).

The Pharisee was thanking God that he needed nothing, so received nothing, but the tax collector begged for mercy. One was satisfied with his own righteousness, but the other received God's righteousness, and went home justified before God. Ironically, at the very moment the Pharisee was thanking God that he wasn't like a tax collector, that tax collector was receiving the forgiveness of sins. While the Pharisee was scorning, the angels were rejoicing.

Thanks!

In September 1860 a Great Lakes steamer, Lady Elgin, floundered in Lake Michigan, near Evanston, Illinois. Nearly 400 perished. Edward W. Spencer, a nearby ministerial student, hearing of the wreck, hurried to the scene and rescued person after person from the sinking boat before he himself fell delirious. Although he recovered, Spencer suffered poor health the rest of his life.

A few decades later, attending a large church service in California, Spencer was called to the platform and recognized as one who had performed so heroically in his youth. Loudly cheered, he sat down. A person nearby asked, "Is there anything special you remember in connection with the seventeen persons you saved from the wreck of the Lady Elgin?" Spencer hesitated a moment, and then said, "Only this, that not one of the seventeen ever thanked me."

Doubtless, all of them were thankful, but not one of them ever looked up the young student who almost lost his life saving them from a watery grave.

Missionary Aviation Fellowship's news publication, *Flight Watch*, tells of MAF's part in fighting leprosy. Through modern science leprosy has been mostly conquered, but it still exists in pockets around the world, affecting up to 10 million. Zimbabwe is such an area. If not caught in time, a victim can no longer do farm work, so critical for survival in rural Africa.

To help fight the malady, an MAF pilot and a missionary doctor, Steve Griffiths, regional director of Leprosy Mission, spend much time together at 8,500 feet in MAF's Cessna. Together they fly to hospitals and leprosy colonies in Zimbabwe and adjacent districts. Without the plane, the doctor would have to rely on ground transportation, which would add days, even weeks to his schedule. The article pointed out the compassion of Jesus for lepers, and the thanks of today's lepers in Africa for MAF's role in enabling doctor and pilot to fight this terrifying disease.

⁂ A Daily Tip   *October 8*

When we travel, my wife has a habit of leaving a daily tip at every lodging. She includes a tract or encouraging Bible verse. Here are some reactions.

A note left by the maid: "To our guests. I praise God that I met a Christian couple. God bless you for sharing the Gospel. I will be ready to share and testify to my cell group that I met you in this hotel. God bless you and your family. Mahalo."

Another note: "I needed those words today. Thank you for the tip also. The Maid."

One maid sent back a note on how much she needed the verse my wife had quoted.

Another maid, a Korean, caught us in the hall returning to our room and asked us to explain the tract. Just then along came a former missionary to Korea, attending the same convention and staying in the room across the hall. He knew her language and said, "They are telling you the same thing I told you about Jesus Christ."

⁂ When the Professor's Pants Fell Down   *October 9*

Dr. Robert Dick Wilson, professor at Princeton Theological Seminary during the early twentieth century, used to come to class with his suspenders held in place by two safety pins. One day the only girl in the class told a boy that she was cutting the class to work on her thesis in the library.

When the girl returned from the library after the class, she passed a group of boys howling with laughter. Professor Wilson had come to class, disheveled and late. He started lecturing, gesticulating wildly. Suddenly the last safety pin popped out of his suspenders. Down came his trousers to the floor. The embarrassed

Thanks!

professor picked up his pants and said, "Where is she?" referring to the only female student in his class. The boys howled. They said, "Don't worry, Dr. Wilson. She cut class to go to the library."

He put up his hands and thankfully exclaimed, "Praise God from whom all blessings flow!"

❧ *October 10*   *Close Calls*

Eight-year-old Ray Linnen was about to cross the street. He decided to wait. A moment later a car sped by, killing three other pedestrians.

In his early 20s, he was working the graveyard shift at a Wichita factory. One morning the relief man came in early and urged Linnen to go home. Making his rounds a few minutes later, the relief man was killed in a boiler explosion.

At 25, on his honeymoon in Colorado, he and his bride crossed a bridge during a ferocious storm. Minutes later floods swept the bridge away.

Driving home one night he decided not to stop at his usual ice cream parlor in Udall, Kansas. Minutes later, a deadly tornado slammed into Udall leveling the ice cream parlor and killing seven inside.

Years later he backed out of a charter flight. The plane crashed, killing 31 people, including 14 Wichita State University football players. Linnen gratefully acknowledges, "God's hand has been in it all."

❧ *October 11*   *Perfect Match*

Rick Jett, pastor of a Wesleyan church in Indiana, had been on kidney dialysis for two years, receiving three treatments a week. At an association dinner in 1998, he was sitting beside a pastor friend, Rev. Gale Janofski, and casually mentioned he was on a waiting list to receive a kidney transplant. Janofski had a strange feeling that the Lord was speaking to him. He prayed about it, discussed it with his wife, and examined his motives. Two days later he walked into Jett's office and offered him a kidney. Said Jett, "It just kind of blew me away. I had been discouraged at the ministerial meeting."

After a battery of tests, Janofski was found to be a perfect match. The transplant was performed in February 1999, and both men have done well. Of course, Jett's thanks to Janofski knows no bounds.

Janofski is also thankful to the Wesleyan denomination and his local church for their support during his recovery before resuming full ministerial duties.

⇒ "Thank You, John"   October 12

The Bible tells the story of four men who banded together to bring a paralyzed man to Jesus. If one of those men had failed to help, the paralytic might never have met the Great Physician.

Sometimes it takes four people to win someone to Jesus. One man said, "It was a combination of my mother, father, youth leader, and my pastor."

Sometimes it takes two or three, or many to win another, or maybe it takes just one. In Louisville, Kentucky, several decades ago, a young Christian won his first convert to Christ. These two fellows lived most of their lives in the same city, and were good friends. The young soul winner, John Broadus, became a seminary professor and authored a classical book on sermon preparation. The other young man became a truck driver, and whenever he met the professor, invariably he touched his hat and said, "Thank you, John. Thank you." Said Dr. Broadus, "I know just what he will say when I meet him coming down the golden street of heaven. It will be just what he said this morning, 'Thank you, John. Thank you!'"

⇒ Flashy or Quiet   October 13

When Benjamin Disraeli married Mrs. Wyndham, the widow of his friend, he did not love her. He married her for money and social status. But in the 33 years that followed, Disraeli became enamored with her and quite devoted to her. Around that time Theodore Roosevelt, a student at Harvard, met Alice Hathaway Lee, the woman who became his wife. It was love at first sight. Disraeli fell in love slowly, but for Roosevelt the experience was sudden.

And so it is with conversion. The Philippian jailer was awakened at midnight by a violent earthquake and dramatically converted (Acts 16:25-34). Earlier in the same chapter we have the conversion story of Lydia, told matter-of-factly and simply, "The Lord opened her heart to respond to Paul's message" (16:14).

To some, conversion comes as a sharp break with the past. To others, conversion is more an enriching and enlarging of the past. Thank God for every conversion, dramatic or routine, flashy or quiet.

≫ *October 14*   **Thank God for Humor**

Comedians use humor as a reaction to the bad news of the day. During the Gulf crisis when Americans needed relief, they made people laugh with jokes about sand and Saddam. When the stock market took a major nose-dive, a comedian joked, "You know, I was talking to my stockbroker today. I said, 'Waiter!'" The line got a huge response. News was bad; people needed relief.

When a news report came out about intoxicated pilots at the controls of commercial airliners, one comedian joked about a pilot who admitted his problem during a flight. After takeoff, at 35,000 feet, he came over the mike, "Hello, this is your pilot speaking. My name is Bob, and I'm an alcoholic."

Humor can relieve tension. An immaculately clean mother spotted a cobweb in her married daughter's kitchen, and asked menacingly, "What's that?" Her daughter quipped, "A science project."

Thank God for tension-busting humor.

⫸ *Thanksgiving Journal*   *October 15*

After left-shoulder surgery my wife, who previously had had a prosthetic replacement for a right shoulder shattered in 28 pieces, and who also had had two broken lumbar vertebrae, received a book from a friend. It was called *Counting My Blessings*. The front cover displayed a dictionary definition of the word "gratitude": "gratis, pleasing, thankful, a feeling of thankful appreciation for favors or benefits received." At the bottom of the cover were these words, "a journal of things to be thankful for."

The journal contained enough pages for well over a year of jotting down reasons for thanks. Each day was headed, "be sure to remember five things to be grateful for every day." She said that by filling in five items each day the journal encouraged her to concentrate on the positive side of her situation, instead of the negative. She observed that when you count your blessings, you don't think about the "lessings" in your life.

⫸ *Blest Be the Tie That Binds*   *October 16*

Theologian Dr. James I. Packer, involved in a scholarly conference, reported that the sessions had tons of fun. At one break the director announced that he had just met a man who had been a husband all his life. The delegates wondered how a man could be a husband before his marriage. "Stand up, Mr. Husband," cried the moderator. And up rose a man with the unlikely name. The conferees whooped and clapped for a half-minute. Humor, commented Packer, provided a safety release from the strain of the sessions.

After a business meeting with several acrimonious debates, rather than using his right to cast the deciding vote, the moderator said, "We need time to rethink the matter. Come back next week, and we'll see if we can break the tie." He announced the closing hymn, "Blest Be the Tie That Binds." They all laughed their way through the song. The following week cool minds were

Thanks!

able to reach an amicable decision.

Thank God for humor that pours oil on troubled churches.

≫ *October 17*   **Thank You, Pastor**

When John Maxwell became senior pastor at Skyline Wesleyan Church near San Diego, a member paid him a visit. "Pastor," said the layman, "I believe God has called me to disciple, encourage, and pray for pastors. And the reason I came here today was so that I could pray for you." Maxwell later admitted, "I wept at the thought of God sending someone just to pray for me." The layman was steadfast in prayer for Maxwell, and during the next 14 years Skyline Wesleyan tripled in size. Maxwell became a national leader in the church growth movement.

Kathy Widenhouse in *Focus on the Family* magazine suggests ways to encourage your pastor, ending with: SAY THANK YOU. "A pastor works in a high-expectation environment in which he is constantly scrutinized and rarely applauded. It costs nothing to say, 'Thank you for everything you are doing. I can see the Lord working through you.' But those words are priceless to your pastor."

≫ *October 18*   **Canine Wisdom**

Sometimes animals show a remarkable sense of loyalty and gratitude, perhaps even greater than humans. I recall a funeral service I was asked to lead. A 15-year-old boy in a nearby town had committed suicide. I did not know the boy nor why I was asked by his mother to preside. What I indelibly remember is what happened at the end of the service. As I walked out of the funeral parlor ahead of the pallbearers and moved toward the hearse, I noticed a dog facing us. He did not bark nor pace, but stood reverently at attention, as the casket was lifted into the hearse. The funeral director whispered to me, "That's the boy's dog."

We all wondered how the dog knew where his master was, and how he found his way there at the proper moment from his home a half mile away to show respect and appreciation. A canine said thanks!

⟫ *Merry Medicine* *October 19*

Medical experts tell us that a person who enjoys a good belly laugh undergoes therapy in many parts of the body. Several laughs equal a good aerobic workout. Such laughing has been called internal jogging. One 17th century preacher listed the three greatest doctors as "Dr. Quiet, Dr. Diet, and Dr. Merryman."

Mark Twain, in *Tom Sawyer*, tells of an old man who, after shaking with laughter from head to foot, remarked that such a laugh was money in his pocket because it cut down the doctor bills.

A doctor said, "If you can't take a joke, you'll have to take medicine." Another parodied, "The surly bird catches the germ." The Bible says, "A cheerful heart is good medicine."

Charles Haddon Spurgeon, prince of preachers, and a friend were walking in the country, laughing and chuckling. When his friend told a story that made them both roar, Spurgeon said, "Let's kneel down and thank God for laughter."

⟫ *Like Clockwork* *October 20*

One author, needing a reminder for periodic meditation, set his watch alarm to chime every hour. He learned later that Benedictine monks used to stop and pray every time the clock chimed.

Brother Lawrence, a cook in a 17th century monastery, in his devotional classic, *The Practice of the Presence of God*, suggested that one way to form the holy habit of thinking of God is to often lift our hearts in thanks for His favors.

Would it not be spiritually healthy to make a determined effort to pause and thank God many times a day—as often as busy computer users check their e-mail? If we say grace at meals, already we have three built-in times a day, and it would help con-

Thanks!

quer the mindless routine, "ThankyouforthisfoodAmen—Please pass the butter." There's so much to thank God for, and we don't have to cry aloud. He's nearer to us than we imagine.

>> *October 21*   **Viewing the World in a New Light**

When Billy Graham was interviewed by Oprah on her TV program, Billy was asked what he was most thankful for. He said, "Salvation given to us in Jesus Christ." Then he added, "And the way you have made people everywhere aware of the power of being grateful."

Oprah devoted an entire issue of her *O* magazine to the topic of thanksgiving. She told how ten years earlier, whining in a difficult time, her mentor insisted, "Stop it right now and say thank you."

So she did—and still does. Only now she does it every day. She keeps a gratitude journal, listing at least five things that she's grateful for.

She says, "It's not easy to feel grateful all the time. Just knowing you have that daily list to complete allows you to look at your day differently, with an awareness of every sweet gesture and kind thought passed your way. When you learn to say thank you, you see the world anew."

>> *October 22*   **The Billboard**

Moishe Rosen, founder of Jews for Jesus, driving east on U.S. Highway 70 in Missouri near the St. Louis airport, saw a billboard with letters so big they filled that whole billboard, but formed just one word—JESUS.

Rosen had this to say to whomever was responsible for the billboard: "Some people would like to accuse you of consummate bad taste, or of forcing your religion upon them—but from the bottom of my heart, I want to thank you because I know that Jesus is the only Name by which men and women might be saved. And when I saw that Name on your billboard, it gave me such a lift.

"As people drive down the highway, most do not want to be bothered about serious things. And somehow, somewhere, someone who doesn't know who Jesus is, is thinking about Him now because of your billboard. Maybe there are several such people, even hundreds. You will never know about them until we all meet in heaven. So, whoever put up that sign, 'Thank you—in Jesus' Name.'"

The Sweetest Name   October 23

Dr. P.W. Philpott, when pastor of Moody Church in Chicago, received a frantic 2 a.m. phone call from a luxury hotel. A young lady was very ill. He went immediately. He led her to trust in Jesus. Next evening, Philpott learned that she and her two in-laws had checked out. He forgot about them.

A few years later Philpott became pastor of the Church of the Open Door in Los Angeles. After a service who should come up to him but the three people whom he had met in the Chicago hotel? Their departure from Chicago had been so sudden they hadn't time to advise him. The past week they had seen his name in a church ad in the newspaper and had come to thank him. The girl was now using her musical talent writing gospel songs. She handed him a manuscript with a new song saying, "I've written this to thank you for introducing me to the Lord Jesus." As Philpott opened the manuscript, he saw the title, "Jesus Is the Sweetest Name I Know," words and music by Lela Long.

The 21st Century, Not the 10th   October 24

According to historians, at the turn of the first millennium life was short. Girls married in their early teens, often to men considerably older than they. Most adults died in their 40s; 50-year-olds were reckoned venerable.

August was the month when flies started to become a problem, buzzing around animal dung heaps in every farmyard, and hovering over the open cesspits of human refuse located outside every house. If the 21st century is scented with gas vapor and exhaust fumes, the 10th century was perfumed with the odor of cow dung, horse manure, pig, sheep and chicken droppings.

The modern cure for fleas—a good bath—was not a common mentality. Monks in one European monastery were required to take five baths per year, but that was considered fanatical. Be thankful you live in the 21st century!

≫ *October 25*   *Coarse, Scratchy, Itchy Clothes*

There were no potatoes or tomatoes in England in A.D. 1000. No broccoli, no cauliflower, no runner beans, nor Brussels sprouts. No spinach. No stimulants yet like tea, coffee, or chocolate.

In an English grave were found the bones of a mother with the skeleton of her baby still inside her, trapped on its way along her birth canal. The woman must have died in the throes of labor without relief of medicine. Nor did she have the opportunity of drastic release by Cesarean section, which is not recorded as being attempted in England until the 16th century.

Since cotton did not exist, imagine wearing scratchy underwear made of coarse, hand-woven wool. Only the wealthy could afford garments of linen, which were woven to a texture that would be too itchy for most modern skins. The industrial revolution would eventually come, making life more bearable, but aren't we thankful we didn't have to live back in the year 1000?

≫ *October 26*   *The Towering Wooden Cross*

On an upper bookshelf in his study, a California pastor kept a little wooden cross. One evening an earthquake struck Long Beach. With the earth still shaking, the pastor made his way through the debris in the street to see the damage in his study. He found hundreds of books stacked high on the floor, plus other articles like lamps and files. He pushed his way through to view the chaos. Squarely on top of all the piled-up books was one with its title showing, *The World in Convulsion*. And standing firmly on this book, absolutely upright, nothing against which to lean, was that little wooden cross. The earth was still trembling, and had been every few minutes since the initial tremor, but there stood that cross.

The pastor burst forth in full voice in thanksgiving, singing the hymn, "In the cross of Christ I glory, Towering o'er the wrecks of time. All the light of sacred history, Gathered round that head sublime."

≫ Tithes and Offerings   *October 27*

Little Nellie was given a new $10 bill. She asked her father to change it into ten $1 bills, explaining, "So I can get the Lord's part out of it, Daddy." When her father gave her ten bills, she took one of the bills and said, "There! I'll keep it till Sunday."

When Sunday came, she went to church and dropped into the offering plate not one dollar, but two dollar bills. Her father was puzzled when he saw the second one drop. "I thought you gave one-tenth to the Lord."

"No, Daddy, I said one-tenth belongs to Him, and I can't give to the Lord what is already His, so if I give Him anything, I must give Him some of the nine-tenths I kept."

Many churches list in the order of worship, "Tithes and offerings." One pastor called the ushers forward to receive "His tithes and our offerings." Gratitude helps develop such an attitude.

≫ Christian Cancellation   *October 28*

A lecturer held up before an audience a large surface of pure white marred by a tiny blot. "What do you see?" he asked. The almost unanimous answer was, "A blot."

How like human nature. We are quick to see the defects in others while failing to note their good qualities. A good way to overcome this tendency is to play the game of Christian cancellation. Here's how: Two boys were speaking of another lad. "He's so slow in baseball," said the first boy. The second replied, "But he always plays fair."

"But he's not very handsome," retorted the first.

"Yes," came the defense, "but he's a whiz at the computer."

Every unkind word spoken by the first boy was canceled by a thankful remark by the second boy.

≫ *October 29*   **The Gift of Blindness**

Songwriter Fanny Crosby, author of more than 8,000 hymns, became blind through a doctor's carelessness when just six. She refused to feel sorry for herself and began composing poetry. She also memorized Bible passages. At 15 she was sent to the New York Institute for the Blind, her home for 13 years.

When Crosby was 30, she dedicated herself to Christ, preferring from then on to write simple verses usable in evangelism like "Blessed Assurance," "Jesus Keep Me Near the Cross," and "All the Way My Savior Leads Me." She harbored no bitterness against the doctor who mistreated her. Rather, she once said, "If I could meet him now, I would say thank you over and over again for making me blind." She felt her blindness was a gift from God to help her write many hymns. Early in life she wrote, "Oh, what a happy soul I am, although I cannot see! I am resolved that in this world, contented I will be."

≫ *October 30*   **Haaaaa-Leeee-Lu-Jaaaaaah**

The little town was excited, for the old man who drove the cattle to market had confessed faith in Christ. Up to now, every morning when the animals did not budge, this infamous sinner exploded with a torrent of blasphemy echoing through the town. How would he get the animals moving now? The big crowd watched as the poor driver, secretly praying, cracked his whip and said, "Getty up!" The animals remained motionless. The whip cracked again and again. One animal turned as if to say, "Old man, we're not used to such gentle words." The people laughed. Any moment the driver would explode.

Praying desperately, the driver cracked his whip and yelled at the top of his voice, "Haaaaa-leeee-lu-jaaaaaah!" The long, drawn-out syllables sounded like a cavalry charge. The beasts lurched forward. The day's work had begun. He kept repeating his inspired command. His "Haaaaa-leeee-lu-jaaaaaahs" won the day. The elated man did his work shouting his praises and thanks to God.

≫ *October 31*   *Deliverance in Time of War*

No nation can remain free from war. Even if it never attacks another country, some designing ruler may launch an unsuspecting attack on its shores, annexing territory, capturing citizens, and bringing major crises to its people. The editors of *The Book of Common Prayer* recognized that victory in war was an occasion for genuine thanksgiving included this collect:

Prayer For Peace, and Deliverance from our Enemies:

O Almighty God, who art a strong tower of defence unto thy servants against the face of their enemies; We yield thee praise and thanksgiving for our deliverance from those great and apparent dangers wherewith we were encompassed. We acknowledge thy goodness that we were not delivered over as a prey unto them; beseeching thee still to continue such thy mercies towards us, that all the world may know that thou art our Saviour and mighty Deliverer; through Jesus Christ our Lord. Amen.

❧ November

During devastating floods in Mozambique in the spring of 2000, a pastor said that for almost two days a group of his members clung to tree limbs to avoid drowning. "The floodwaters came so quickly," he told Tearfund, a British evangelical relief agency. "I helped some people onto the roof of my house and then we climbed a tree. We saw televisions, furniture, and dead calves float past. Everything in my house was destroyed."

As the hours wore on, the people asked the pastor to preach to help them stay awake. But even the minister was having trouble. Just then, mosquitoes began swarming and biting.

"I thank God for those mosquitoes because they stopped me (and the others) from falling asleep. If we had fallen asleep we would have been carried away by the water." When the floodwaters receded, the group was able to wade to safety.

❧ *November 2* **All She Didn't Have**

Barbara Curtis said that after years of thanking God it was time to be grateful for all she didn't have—for some past deprivations. She mentions not having a full refrigerator and missing meals as a child. That memory makes it easy to give to a hungry man or woman.

She's grateful for the stability she never had as a child. Though divorce, foster homes, frequent moves and separations were hard on her, they did make her appreciate the strong family foundation she and her husband have laid. Not having a dependable earthly father makes her heavenly Father all the more wonderful.

Their hasty marriage as New Agers drove them to a Christian marriage conference and a commitment of their lives to Christ. Their son with Down syndrome has opened parts of their hearts they never knew were there.

She concludes, "Now I couldn't imagine having lived without any of the parts of my life—even those that seemed bad and ugly. For every part, I give thanks."

≫ For the Harvest — *November 3*

From *The Book of Common Prayer:*
Thanks for Rain:
O God, our heavenly Father, by whose gracious providence the former and the latter rain descend upon the earth, that it may bring forth fruit for the use of man; We give thee humble thanks that it hath pleased thee to send us rain to our great comfort, and to the glory of thy holy Name; through Jesus Christ our Lord. Amen.

Thanks for Plenty:
O most merciful Father, who of thy gracious goodness hast heard the devout prayers of thy Church, and turned our dearth and scarcity into plenty; We give thee humble thanks for this thy special bounty; beseeching thee to continue thy loving-kindness unto us, that our land may yield us her fruits of increase, to thy glory and our comfort; through Jesus Christ our Lord. Amen.

≫ Just Thoughtless — *November 4*

Jesus once cured ten lepers but only one returned to give thanks. Ten outcasts who could never go home to wife and children, disfigured, with scaly skin, shunned by all and forced to beg outside city gates, suddenly healed! Wouldn't gratitude force

Thanks!

them to run back to their benefactor and fall at His feet? But only one returned.

The Lord knew exactly how many failed to return thanks. He asked, "Where are the nine?" None of us is lost in a crowd to Him. He is fully aware of every individual who has never specifically acknowledged the supreme gift of His sacrificial death on the cross, and is grieved by such neglect.

Those nine were not maliciously unthankful. They would not have denied their debt to Jesus; they just never thought to thank Him. Repeatedly, by parable and plain statement, Jesus warned against thankless indifference to the divine invitation. Paul described mankind in its natural state as "ungrateful" (2 Tim. 3:2).

May God cure us from thoughtlessness!

⠀November 5   *Sign Language*

A mother's unusual decision to teach her 3-old daughter sign language may have saved the mother's life. One February afternoon in 2005, Kristin Comeau began to cough uncontrollably and have difficulty breathing. The Long Island mother dialed 911, but when the operator answered, as she opened her mouth to speak, her throat closed up and she couldn't get any words out. Comeau, who had taught her daughter sign language as a hobby, then signed the word "help" to her daughter, and the girl repeated it to the 911 operator. The little girl also gave the operator her address, as her father had taught her. Comeau was taken to a hospital, where she recovered from what was diagnosed as a severe allergic reaction.

"I couldn't believe how well she did," Comeau told a reporter. Though she had no particular reason to teach her daughter sign language, she is so thankful she did. Now she's also teaching her younger son sign language.

≫ *The Grumblers* *November 6*

The Grumbler Song, popular a few decades back, began: "In country, town or city, some people can be found who spend their lives in grumbling at everything around; O yes, they always grumble, no matter what we say, For these are chronic grumblers and they grumble night and day . . . ."

In an area in Mexico hot and cold springs are close together where tourists can watch women boiling their clothes in a hot spring, then rinsing them in a cold one nearby. One tourist remarked, "I suppose these women are thankful." The guide replied, "No, senor, they grumble because there's no soap."

A man dissatisfied with his small estate hired an agent to write an ad describing the estate. When the agent read the ad to him, the owner commented, "I don't think I'll sell after all. I've been looking for an estate like that, and didn't know I already own it."

Grumbling overlooks blessings for which we should give thanks.

≫ *"I Can Hardly Keep From Telling You"* *November 7*

If you were given ten minutes' warning before sudden death, ten minutes to say what life had meant to you, every cell phone would be pulled out, every telephone booth would be occupied, every computer would be sending e-mails by people trying to reach family and friends to stammer that they loved them, or to say, "I appreciate you so much. I want to thank you for all you've done for me."

Up in Vermont, an old farmer was sitting on the porch with his wife. He was beginning to realize how much she meant to him. They had lived together 42 years. She had been such a help. After a little more inner reminiscing, he remarked, "Mary, you've been such a wonderful woman that there are times I can hardly keep from telling you."

Thanks!

We ought often to express our gratitude for others. Paul wrote to his friend, Philemon, "I always thank my God as I remember you in my prayers" (v. 4).

≫ *November 8*   ***Six Times—Maybe Seven***

Six times in Colossians (95 verses) Paul mentions thanks:

1:3. Paul follows his opening greeting with thanks for their faith, love, and hope.

1:12. Paul rejoices that a thankful spirit accompanies their worthy walk.

2:7. Paul urges his readers to the duty of "overflowing with thankfulness," the natural expression of a faith rooted in Christ.

3:15. "Let the peace of Christ rule in your hearts . . . . And be thankful." Don't fail to be grateful. Cultivate this virtue.

3:17. Paul reaches the climax of his general exhortations, adding, ". . . giving thanks to God the Father through him."

4:2. Prayer must be accompanied by gratitude.

A possible 7th reference to thanks in Colossians is in the NIV (3:16) which reads, "sing . . . with gratitude in your hearts to God." The Greek word used generally means "grace," but sometimes it can mean "thanks."

≫ *November 9*   ***Not by Chance***

Some cannibals caught a missionary. A big, boiling pot began to steam not far away. "Going to eat me?" the missionary asked. "Why don't you taste me to see if you'll like me?" Whereupon he sliced a piece from the calf of his leg and gave it to the chief, who took one bite, made a face, and almost choked. The missionary worked on that island for 30 more years. He had a cork leg. He could now thank God for a childhood accident that required the amputation of his leg. Till then he had never realized it would mean the survival of his missionary career years later.

A man was driving his car down the highway near the end of a business trip. Falling drowsy, he began to swerve a little off the road. At that moment, a bird flew in the driver's window, struck the driver on the forehead, alerting him in the nick of time. He often wondered why a sparrow would be flying around at 1 a.m. Now he understood and appreciated the divine wisdom.

With God things just don't happen by chance.

❧ *False Prophets*   *November 10*

In 2000 The Rockland (New York) Historical Society printed excerpts from two Nyack papers dated December 1908, to show that wild millennial predictions were nothing new. Both papers told of a prophecy by a Leo J. Spangler, "the great American seer," who had invited Nyack folks "to climb to the hill in South Nyack and join with the saints on Sunday next, when the world will be no more." Hundreds were expected by train at this town 20 miles north of New York.

The Monday papers reported that three of Spangler's local followers, all in white dresses, were seated in the station. Curious locals strolled nearby. When the train came in, no saints were aboard. The three saints started slowly toward the cemetery atop the hill. People peeped from behind curtains. The cemetery superintendent, annoyed with people walking over graves, asked the saints in white to leave. Big disappointment was the non-appearance of the "prophet" Spangler himself, who promised to prophesy more later.

Thank God for Church leaders who hold sane views on Jesus' Return.

❧ *Veterans Day*   *November 11*

A retired U.S. Air Force major used to visit veterans in nursing homes around his state. He thought veterans were regularly remembered, especially on Memorial Day and Veterans Day, but found this was not the case. These men and women who sacrificed so much to bring peace to our country seem to have been forgotten and ignored, and their sacrifices unappreciated by the general population.

The major always wore his uniform. When one veteran, who had not spoken for four months, saw the uniform, he sat upright in bed and his eyes lit up. The major gave him an American flag as an expression of his gratitude. The veteran took the flag, held it to his lips, grabbed the major's hand, and said, "Thank you, thank you." There wasn't a dry eye in the room.

Often quiet heroes shared cherished memories with the major. Over and over their families tell how much they appreciated his interest and how much his simple expression of respect meant to the veterans.

≫ *November 12*   **Noah's Ark**

When my wife and I were on a trip, she spotted a handmade wooden Noah's ark. She bought it and displayed it in our family room. Soon her friends began to give us more arks and Noahs, as well as other ark trivia—ornaments, jewelry, dishes, towels, hangings, a purse, a clock, ties, books, a bank, even a truck. Needless to say, she has quite an extensive collection. It seems people take a special delight in finding or making unusual Noah's ark items and bringing or sending them here. (Were they hinting I was Noah and 600 years old?)

One editor, hearing she was an authority on Noah's ark, phoned her to ask some questions. She is no expert but does appreciate Noah. When I retired, to distinguish the church property we continue to live in from the new parsonage, she answered the phone with the greeting, "Noah's ark!" Our personal stationery included in our return address, "Noah's ark." We used an e-mail password for one of our family computers: "Noahsark."

My wife reminded me that after the flood Noah built an altar (first mention of an altar in the Bible) and sacrificed some of all the clean animals and birds, an expansive offering of grateful and adoring sentiments to God for His goodness and grace (Gen. 8:20).

⋙ Thankful Quietude   *November 13*

When I was a student for the ministry in Chicago, I had an
assignment which took me into rural Indiana every weekend. I
noticed the quiet of the country town in contrast to the noise of
the city. My school was located on a busy Chicago corner. Every
night a cacophony of sound rang out: the clanging of street cars,
the sirens of ambulances, fire trucks, and police cars, the swish of
traffic, and the racket of Chicago's elevated commuter train. The
noise lulled me to sleep.

But in the country I had a hard time getting to sleep—the
silence was thunderous. If I made the effort, I could hear chirping
birds, buzzing bees, cooing pigeons, and other auditory pleasures
of God's creation, for which we should take time to give thanks.

A jukebox permits people to hear a favorite tune belted out.
Wouldn't it be wonderful if jukeboxes listed "silence" as one
of the choices, permitting the option of five minutes of thankful
quietude?

⋙ Face to Face   *November 14*

As the sun was setting early one evening at a Poughkeepsie,
New York, camp meeting, several guests were sitting on the hotel
porch, among them a preacher and the blind hymnwriter Fanny
Crosby. As the sky began to glow in splendor, the preacher
described to Fanny the brilliance as the colors formed into great
shafts of light. She hung on his every adjective. When he finished,
Fanny thanked him for the strength it had given her as it revived
memories of the sunsets her grandmother used to describe to her
as a little girl. As she rose to go inside the hotel, she said to the
preacher, "Though I cannot now see the sunset, someday I'll see
my Savior face to face!"

Before the camp meeting ended, Fanny composed a poem
which, later put to music, began: "Some day the silver cord will
break, And I no more as now shall sing; But O the joy when I shall

wake, Within the palace of the King! And I shall see Him face to face, And tell the story, Saved by grace."

☙ *November 15*   *A Universal Thanks*

Thanking God should lead to praising God. "Praise the Lord" occurs 13 times in Psalm 150, at least twice in each of the six verses, summoning all voices and instruments in one grand finale of the entire Psalter.

What. "Praise the Lord" means "Hallelujah," a word used by the Church universal, and sung by the heavenly host (Rev. 19).

Where. Indoors, in the sanctuary. Also outdoors, in sky and nature.

Why. First, for His acts of power. Second, for His surpassing greatness. Praise Him for His works and person, what He does and who He is.

How. Half of the Psalm is taken up with ways to praise Him. The mention of cymbals comes last, perhaps as the instrument most expressive of jubilation.

Who. Voices are to be added to the instruments, bringing to a climax this thunder-chorus of praise to Jehovah. All kinds of instruments are to be joined by all kinds of people, prefiguring a day when all creatures worship Jehovah.

☙ *November 16*   *Wrapping a Gift With a Smile*

The thought of an offering pains some people. During a revival meeting a man, stirred by the message, began to shout loudly, "Praise the Lord! Amen! That's right, brother!" Every few moments he repeated some exclamation to the point of annoyance. The preacher, wanting to end the disturbance, and knowing the offender's reputation for stinginess, waited for a moment of silence, then quietly announced, "I feel led to stop preaching right now and take a missionary offering. I'd like to invite all of you folks who love the Lord and who like to express your love for Him to give generously." The shouting stopped. The man reached for his hat and slipped out.

The Old Testament called on God's people to "Give generously to him and do so without a grudging heart . . ." (Deut. 15:10). An extra-canonical book advised, "With every gift show a cheerful face . . ." (Ecclesiasticus 35:9).

A thankful heart will help wrap a gift with a smile.

⟫ Salty Soup   *November 17*

In a certain lumber camp nobody wanted to do the cooking because the lumberjacks were so insulting about the food. Someone would shout out, "What kind of soup is this? It tastes like kerosene."

One day the foreman decided to appoint someone. "John, you'll be the next cook, but the first one who objects to the food will have to take over the cooking." John cooked for a week, then a whole month, and nobody complained. One day, because John was tired of doing the cooking, he thought he would give them a reason to complain by dumping all the salt in the soup. He shouted, "Come and get it!" The first fellow took a spoonful, and yelled, "Boy, is this soup salty!" Then he immediately realized his mistake and sputtered out, "But I'm so thankful because this is just the way I like it."

If there were some penalty for forgetting to say thanks, perhaps our diligence to say thanks would make our home, workplace, neighborhood, and church a better place.

⟫ God's Providence   *November 18*

The lone survivor of a shipwreck, marooned on an uninhabitable island, managed to build a hut in which he placed his few belongings. Daily he prayed for rescue and scanned the horizon for sight of a passing ship he might signal. One day on returning from a hunt for food he was horror-stricken to find his hut in flames. All his possessions gone up in smoke! The rest of the day he bemoaned his loss. But next morning he thanked God when he saw a ship arrive. "We saw your smoke signal yesterday," the captain explained.

Someone said, "Accidents do not happen. What seems an accident today may prove a blessing tomorrow. What we deem an accident unplanned by man is in reality an incident planned by God, which the skillful weaver is intertwining into a lovely pattern without a thread or color out of place."

A thankful spirit helps us believe all things work together for good and that when a mishap comes, "behind a frowning providence he hides a smiling face."

≫ *November 19*   Seeing the Sunny Side

Someone said, "An optimist may be wrong as often as a pessimist, but he is far happier." Part of that happier outlook stems from gratitude. Two boys were gathering grapes. One was grateful there were so many. The other discovered the grapes contained seeds, and moaned. Two girls saw a bright, green bush. One was thankful for its lovely roses. The other noticed the thorns and complained. Two men conversed on a rainy day. One appreciated the needy rain. The other growled about the weather.

Thanking forestalls complaining. Winston Churchill used to tell about a picnic where a five-year-old boy fell into the lake, but was rescued at great risk by a passerby. The mother, instead of thanking the stranger for his brave act, snapped at the hero, "Where's Johnny's cap?" Discontent "makes men's lips like rusty hinges, seldom to move without murmuring and carping."

Gratitude helps us "Do everything without complaining or arguing" (Phil. 2:14).

≫ *O Death, Where Is Thy Sting?*   *November 20*

My wife relates the following story: "In college I became close friends with Grace Rice, eldest daughter of a well-known evangelist. We shared hopes and article ideas. Grace was a bridesmaid at my wedding. But then our paths separated. One day I learned she was seriously ill with cancer. I called her in Texas and was amazed to hear her joyful voice. She said she had been busy giving talks to Women's Jubilee groups and editing the magazine, *The Joyful Woman*. She was thankful for all of God's goodness. I thought, 'Grace, you are dying. Your life is over. I wonder if I were hit with a death sentence, could I be so resilient?'

"Later her husband sent me a tape of her victorious funeral service, and told how on her deathbed she had been planning messages for another Women's Jubilee."

Someone said, "God is glorified not by our groans but by our thanks."

⋙ *A Full Thanksgiving*   *November 21*

The apostle Paul, near the end of his life, languished in a Roman prison, likely the dreaded Mammertine dungeon (2 Tim. 4:6-18). He asked Timothy to bring him certain items that reflect his thankfulness to God.

Something for the body. ". . . bring the cloak that I left with Carpus at Troas," to protect him from the cold, damp jail, and to "Get here before winter."

Something for the mind. Paul wanted "my scrolls, especially the parchments." What wonderful friends books can be! When Tyndale was detained in a Belgium castle, he wanted a warmer cap and a Hebrew Bible.

Something for our social nature. "Get Mark and bring him with you." Cloaks and books are not enough. Paul needed his friends.

Something for the spirit. Paul wrote that at first no one came to his support. "But the Lord stood at my side and gave me strength."

Covering for the body, cultivation for the mind, companionship for the soul, and the comfort of Christ, a full thanksgiving indeed.

Thanks!

After the suffering of difficult years, an early colony in New England gathered a modest harvest. But some leaders had doubts about the winter ahead, so they called a day of fasting and confession of the community's shortcomings. The meeting droned on till finally a little man strode up front, and said, "I must dissent. I've heard enough of sin and doom." A gasp of surprise went through the room. The man continued, "I have fasted till my stomach rebelled. I have meditated on my sins till my mind was reeling. Now I must lift my eyes and thank the good Lord for the things we have! And let us end this pointless fasting!"

A murmur filled the room. The more eloquent confessors looked humbled. Within an hour the fireplace was lit, meat was provided, and pots were simmering. By sundown the day of fasting and mourning had become a day of feasting and merriment, as thanksgiving saturated the settlement.

An emcee at a Thanksgiving banquet introduced the speaker thus: "Ladies and gentlemen, you have been focusing your attention on turkey stuffed with sage. Now it's my privilege to present to you a sage stuffed with turkey."

Though Thanksgiving Day is observed nationally only once a year, thanksgiving should be given at every meal, even if quietly.

Mary Lou Retton, Olympic gold-winner in gymnastics at Los Angeles in 1984, says that she and her husband have tried to teach their daughters that thanking God for the gift of food is not something you do only on special occasions like Thanksgiving. "We should be equally grateful for the breakfast, lunch, and dinner we eat every day of the week. We don't always have to say grace when we're going through the drive-through at McDonald's, but a silent prayer of thanks seems like the least we can do to show appreciation for the food we eat when so many people in the world have less."

⫸ *A Lifetime of Thanksgiving* *November 24*

Time has abbreviated our expression of appreciation. First it was a full "I thank you." A faster tempo of life shortened it to, "Thank you." Still later it became just, "Thanks." Then later, many times no thanks at all, or perhaps a casual tip-of-the-hat to gratitude on Thanksgiving Day, sitting down with this wish:

May your stuffing be tasty, May your turkey be plump,
May your potatoes n' gravy Have nary a lump,
May your yams be delicious, May your pies take the prize,
May your Thanksgiving dinner Stay off your thighs!

Thanksgiving shouldn't be limited to an annual holiday with the thought of turkey and football. Thanksgiving should be a way of life.

⫸ *The First Thanksgiving* *November 25*

Barbara Curtis sums up the story of the first Thanksgiving. A group of Separatists, persecuted for forming a church outside the Church of England, settled in Holland, then sailed for the New World. On the Mayflower they were joined by others seeking the new land for other reasons, called the "Strangers." These two groups totaled 102 and together were called "Pilgrims." The voyage lasted nine weeks, during which the ship lost its course and instead of reaching Virginia, landed at Cape Cod in 1620. Half the Pilgrims died the first winter. But, clinging to their faith in God, not one of the survivors returned to England the next spring when the Mayflower sailed back.

Aided by an Indian, Squanto, the first harvest brought plenty. In October the governor set aside a day for all to feast and thank God for meeting their needs. For political correctness some recent books teach that the Pilgrims offered the first Thanksgiving to thank the Indians or Mother Earth. But the original Thanksgiving was really a day of lifting up thanks to God Almighty.

Thanks!

Martin Rinckart took up a pastorate in Eilenberg, Germany, in 1618 just as the Thirty Years' War began. Some believe this was the most devastating war in history with Germany's population dropping from 16 million to 6 million. Because Eilenberg was a walled city, refugees from all over the country sought haven there, many bringing diseases to the crowded city. The plague of 1637 ravaged the community. With Rinckart the only pastor left in town, that year he conducted over 5,000 funerals, including his wife's. During the dreadful thirty-year conflict he wrote this well-known thanksgiving hymn which begins:

> Now thank we all our God with heart and hands and voices,
> Who wondrous things hath done, in whom his world rejoices.

In the midst of great suffering, he still thanked God for the power of His help.

A woman, widowed and penniless, walked wearily into a grocery store in West Chicago. "I have nothing to offer but a little prayer," she said, handing a piece of paper over the counter, "I wrote out my prayer last night, watching my sick baby."

Customers were watching. The embarrassed grocer, placing the paper on one side of his old-fashioned scales, said, "Let's see how much food this prayer is worth." He placed a loaf of bread on the other side. Nothing happened. More food was added several times, until the scale would hold no more. The grocer was astonished, confused and angry. He studied the dial of the scales, but the needle still pointed to zero. Flustered, he gave her a big sack of food. After she was gone, he looked the scales over and found they were broken. They had worked till the moment the woman walked in.

The clerk snatched the little scrap of paper and read what she had written. "Please, Lord, give us this day our daily bread."

❧ *A Cheerful Giver* *November 28*

Before a missionary offering, these resolutions were adopted: (1) That we will all give. (2) That we will give as the Lord has prospered us. (3) That we will give cheerfully (2 Cor. 9:7).

Each person walked forward individually. When one rich member finally came forward to deposit his gift, the presiding officer said, "That is according to the first resolution, but not according to the second." The member returned indignantly to his seat, taking back his money. Under pressure he came forward again, doubling his contribution, muttering, "Take that, then." The presiding officer commented, "That may meet the first and second resolutions, but isn't according to the third." Again the giver retired to his seat where he did some thinking—and thanking. A few minutes later he came up the third time with a still larger gift and a good-natured smile and a thankful heart. Then the chairman exclaimed, "That's according to all resolutions."

Unless giving flows from thanks, it's not thanksgiving!

❧ *Unfeigned Thanks* *November 29*

From *The Book of Common Prayer:*
At End of Day:

To our prayers, O Lord, we join our unfeigned thanks for all thy mercies . . . for our being, our reason, and all other endowments and faculties of soul and body; for our health, friends, food, and raiment, and all the other comforts and conveniences of life. Above all, we adore thy mercy in sending thy only Son into the world, to redeem us from sin and eternal death, and in giving us the knowledge and sense of our duty towards thee. We bless thee for thy patience with us, notwithstanding our many and great provocations; for thy watchful providence over us through the whole course of our lives; and particularly for the mercies and benefits of the past day . . . and humbly supplicate thy merciful protection all this night. Bring us, in safety to the morning hours;

Thanks!

through him who died for us and rose again, thy Son, our Savior Jesus Christ. Amen.

≫ *November 30*   **The One Who Died for Another**

During World War II, Frank Gajowniczek, a sergeant in the Polish Army, was captured by the Nazis and sent to Auschwitz. In July 1941 some prisoners escaped. In retaliation the Nazis arbitrarily selected ten innocent victims to die by starvation. Among the ten was Gajowniczek, who cried out "Have mercy! I have a wife and children! I want to live to see them." A moment later a man stepped forward. He was a priest, Maxmillian Kolbe, captured by the Gestapo a few months before. He told the commandant that he was willing to take the place of the man who had a family. The commandant, amazed at such compassion, permitted the exchange. The priest joined the other nine and died. The soldier was released to rejoin his wife and children.

For years Sergeant Gajowniczek made a yearly pilgrimage to Auschwitz to place a wreath on Father Kolbe's grave, the man who died in his place. Have you thanked Jesus for dying in your place?

❧ December

A man lived with his wife and six children in Philadelphia. As school opening neared, all six were in need of new shoes. At the same time the washing machine stopped working. Answering an ad from a party with a used washing machine, he found himself in a home filled with the comforts of life. After he made arrangements to pick up the old washer, the conversation with the man and lady of the house got around to children. He commented on the problems of feeding and clothing six children. The woman ran out of the room crying. The father explained that they had only one child who had been paralyzed from birth and had never needed a pair of shoes.

When the buyer of the washing machine reached home, he said, "I picked the worn-out shoes, worn out from skipping rope, kicking rocks, and jumping puddles. My wife and I knelt by our bed and thanked God for the worn-out shoes in our house."

❧ *Personal Thanks* *December 2*

Etiquette consultants have noticed a slippage of proper expression of gratitude in various social situations. At the end of a news article on the marriage of a local couple was this postscript, "In lieu of sending personal thank-you notes for wedding gifts, the couple made a donation to the American Cancer Society." A manners expert commented, "This practice is an attempt to escape the tedious job of writing thank-you notes, and

Thanks!

is unacceptable."

At a wedding, guests were handed a printed thank-you note, and gift-givers were told that they would receive no other thanks. Inadequate.

One lady lamented that twice she had received from a high school graduate a note embossed, "Thank you from the Graduate," simply signed by the graduate on the inside. She commented, "This hurried note is only better than nothing. I was taught to personalize the note by making mention of the specific gift in my own writing. That's what I did at both my graduation and wedding."

Personal thanks means a lot—that someone noticed and cares and appreciates someone else's thoughtfulness.

≫ *December 3*   **Daily Bread**

When an airplane plant closed down on Long Island, an electronics engineer tried to find work, but without success. He sent his resume to company after company. No one was hiring. The couple was now down to their last can of noodle soup. As was their custom, they bowed to pray the Lord's Prayer. The husband was a bread man, enjoying eating bread with soup, but today there was no bread. They reached the line, "Give us this day our daily bread."

Just then came an insistent knocking at the back door. They hurried through the rest of the prayer; then the wife answered the door. The husband heard a neighbor say, "Can you use any bread? My brother is a route man for a big company. They're giving out sample loaves. He has four cases left and can't bring them back. I've taken two and can't fit any more in my house. Can you use the other two?"

Husband and wife were astonished and so thankful. They now had bread for soup, bread for sandwiches, bread for toast, bread for dinner, bread for a late snack, bread for bread pudding, bread for everything!

☲≫ *Operation Christmas Child* *December 4*

On a Sunday in December, dedicated by church elders to Operation Christmas Child, a ministry of Franklin Graham's Samaritan's Purse, Calvary Chapel in Albuquerque, New Mexico, collects over 15,000 shoeboxes of gifts and goods every year. Graham, visiting there one year, tells the story of a woman who brought a packed box. When she was in a refugee camp in Bosnia in the early 1990s, someone gave her a shoebox. For the first time in her life, as a young girl, she experienced a little joy and hope that someone loved her. Now attending the University of Mexico, she has come to know Jesus Christ as her personal Savior and was giving her own Christmas shoebox to help a child.

Graham also tells of a Muslim family in Beirut who was searching for a copy of a children's Bible. They had seen another family with such a copy and wanted one for their son. When Operation Christmas Child did a distribution of shoeboxes in a Lebanese school, that little boy opened his shoebox and found a copy of the Bible in the Arabic language. Graham says, "When I hear stories like these, I cannot help but say, 'Thank You, Father!'"

☲≫ *Only Dutch* *December 5*

Pam Hogan learned to speak Dutch fluently while attending Dutch schools on the island of Bonaire where her parents were missionaries. Even as a girl before she left the island, she wondered if she would ever be able to use the language, especially after enrolling in a California college.

One day Pat heard someone in the crowd of students behind her mention "Dutch." A student explained, "An elderly lady nearby is very ill and needs care. But she speaks only Dutch. She used to speak English also, but she's had several strokes and forgotten it. Her name is Corrie ten Boom." As a girl, Pam had met this famous lady, who had provided a hiding place for Jews in Holland during the Holocaust. Now, aged and ill, she had need of special

Thanks!

care which Pam was uniquely qualified to give. Pam was hired to sit by Corrie two or three evenings a week and turn her frail frame hourly. She kept this vigil for over a year. How thankful Pam was for proficiency in a second language.

≫ *December 6*   ***Pastor Appreciation***

Urging parishioners to show appreciation in a tangible way, the general director of one denomination wrote in its church paper, "Have you ever provided a relaxing respite for one of your pastors or busy ministry leaders? Arranging for a two-day mini-vacation at a nice hotel, a dinner-for-two gift certificate, tickets to a ball game, or a day alone for a couple with baby-sitting provided are some examples of what can be done." He cited the model of Onesiphorus who found ways to refresh the apostle Paul, once traveling over 800 miles to Rome to diligently search for him till he found him (2 Tim. 1:16-17).

A respected pastor in England, depressed, was walking down a street. He was greeted by a poor lady he did not recognize. "God bless you, Pastor. If you could only know how many times you have helped me, and what a happy home you have given me—God bless you!" The pastor said the sun broke though the fog of his depression so he could breathe again. Appreciation is good medicine.

≫ *December 7*   ***A Bombardier's Bitterness***
___

Japanese Air Commander Captain Mitsuo Fuchida led the attack on Pearl Harbor in 1941. Years later came reports of Captain Fuchida's conversion. I invited him to speak in our church in March 1967. He gave his story.

As he was getting off a train in Tokyo someone handed him a tract entitled, "I Was a Prisoner of Japan." It was written by an American named Jacob DeShazer, a bombardier on Doolittle's surprise raid on Tokyo, whose bomber ran out of fuel over China. Parachuting to safety, DeShazer became a prisoner of Japan. Soon he became embittered as he remained a prisoner for 40 long, cruel months. But through a Bible he found Christ in the prison camp. He promised God that, if he survived, he would return to Japan as a missionary. And he did.

Said Fuchida, "DeShazer's tract inspired me to get a Bible. I read it day after day until I came to the story of Jesus on the cross. At that moment I accepted Him as my personal Savior. I thank God for sending His only Son to die for my sins. He has truly changed my bitter heart into a loving one."

⇨ Michael Jordan's Memories   *December 8*

Mary Lou Retton first met Michael Jordan at the Olympic Games in Los Angeles in 1984, when she won the gold medal in the women's gymnastics. Jordan, a very talented basketball player from North Carolina, also won a gold medal that year.

In 1996, when Mary Lou was writing her column for *USA Today* at the Summer Olympics in Atlanta, Michael told her about the need for appreciating our loved ones while we can. Michael had recently lost his father in a horrible tragedy. Two young men shot him in cold blood on a major Southern highway to steal his car. She asked Michael how he dealt with the pain and the loss. She said she'll never forget his answer: "From the death of my father, I took a positive view. Hey, I had him for thirty-one years. Some people never had their father for two or three years. He was able to mold me into a mature young man who could make decisions for myself."

How good to be able to say, "Thanks for the memories."

⇨ An Examination Prayer   *December 9*

Dr. P.B. Fitzwater, esteemed professor at Moody Bible Institute, Chicago, taught the doctrine courses required of all students. He headed the Pastors' Department and taught theology, homiletics, and preaching as well. Dr. Fitzwater would always offer the following prayer year after year before the midterm and

Thanks!

final examination of his various courses:

"Thank you, Lord, for the privilege of studying this subject.
As we come now to the examination, please grant us:
  calmness of spirit,
  retentiveness of memory,
  keenness of intellect,
  and facility of expression.
        —in Christ's name."

Thousands of students owe a big "thank you" to Dr. Fitzwater, not only for his intellect and teaching skills, but also for his Examination Prayer.

❧ *December 10*   *Reflection on God's Mercies*

At pivotal points in Israel's history, leaders reviewed God's gracious dealings on their behalf. This rehearsal of divine goodness was designed to evoke thankfulness and obedience. To a new generation about to enter the Promised Land, Moses recounted God's magnificent miracles performed for their forefathers (Deut. 11:1-7).

In his final charge to the people of Israel, Joshua reviewed the history of God's mercies. Because of His abounding goodness they were urged to choose "this day" whom they would serve— God or worthless idols (Josh. 24:14-15).

In the Gospels, the woman who washed Jesus' feet with her tears and wiped them with her hair had a deep understanding of the extent of his forgiveness. The host, Simon the Pharisee, had much less appreciation, if any, so showed little gratitude. Jesus said, "Her many sins have been forgiven—for she loved much. But he who has been forgiven little loves little" (Luke. 7:47).

Reflection on God's grace makes us say, "How much I owe!"

❧ *December 11*   *Now Is the Day of Thanksgiving*

One night an old fisherman heard a splash in the river. Suspecting a drunken fisherman had fallen overboard, he soon made out the struggling form, pulled him up, and rowed the inebriated sailor to his own boat, then left. Next morning the old fisherman saw the alcoholic leaning over the side of his boat. "How are you this morning?" he asked.

"What's that to you?" came the gruff reply.

"I was interested," said the old fisherman, "because last night I fished you out of the river and saved your life." The alcoholic cursed him over and over, and called him a liar. His rescuer, deeply grieved, rowed away. Then he realized he knew something of the grief felt by Jesus when people act as if He never died on the cross to save them. To fail to thank Him is an insult. Some day it will be too late to thank Jesus Christ for dying for us. Now is the day of thanksgiving.

≫ A Thank-You Note and a Gift Package　December 12

In 1984 Tim Botts, Tyndale House's first inhouse artist, began his project of reading through the entire Bible with a sketchbook handy. The result was *Doorposts*, a book with 400 calligraphic renderings of Bible texts.

A copy was sent to the widow of his mentor, calligraphy professor Arnold Bank. Months passed without acknowledgment. But then a package came which included a thank-you note explaining that she had been visiting relatives in Israel. In the package was something Bank's widow had found in Israel to celebrate Botts' title—a parchment inscribed with Deuteronomy 6:4-9 rolled up in a container used by many Jewish households to attach it to their door frames. Botts redesigned his artwork on *Doorposts* so that the words from Deut. 6:5 formed an elegantly arched doorway: "Love the Lord your God with all your heart, all your soul, and all your strength." In February 2000 the artwork took the prize at the annual calligraphy exhibit at Chicago's Newberry Library.

Chief requisite for an ungrateful heart is a poor memory. The many plagues on Israel during its wilderness wanderings resulted from Israel's failure to think of God's miraculous help in days past. "They forgot what he had done, the wonders he had shown them" (Ps. 78:11), and so lapsed into idolatry and numerous sins. So God's judgment fell.

King Hezekiah, miraculously healed of serious illness and given fifteen extra years of life, "did not respond to the kindness shown him" (2 Chron. 32:25). Full of pride, he made a vain display of his riches, later bringing wrath on him and on Judah and Jerusalem. Admittedly, this seems to be the lone lapse in his otherwise long list of good and wise deeds and unblemished loyalty to Jehovah.

Jesus spoke of a rich fool who thought full barns guaranteed a rosy future, but forgot that each day was a gift from God (Luke 12:16-21).

Let us never forget all God's goodness and gifts.

☙ *December 14*   **True Appreciation**

"True Appreciation," a poem by Levi A. Lovegren, retired Baptist missionary who spent several years as a prisoner in a World War II internment camp, says it all:

He, who never lacked for food and often has been overfed,
Little can appreciate plain, simple food as daily bread.
He, who never suffered thirst, nor wandered out in desert
   waste,
Little can appreciate pure water's very pleasant taste.
He, who never has been ill, nor ever suffered wound
   nor burn,
Little can appreciate Good health, which lost, may not return.
He, who always has been free, and never sat in prison cell,
Little can appreciate the Liberty we love so well.
He, who always stayed at home and never left our

freedom's land,
Little can appreciate what we've received at Freedom's hand!

⇛ On the Moon   *December 15*

Astronaut Scott Carpenter, after circling the earth in space, said, "the colors glowed vigorously, alive with light, leaving only a rim of blue." He said the event was all but supernatural.

Neil Armstrong and Buzz Aldrin made the initial moon landing on July 20, 1969. In a book twenty years later, *Men From Earth,* Aldrin describes a not too widely publicized incident that occurred soon after the two astronauts in the lunar module, Eagle, landed on the moon's Sea of Tranquility. Before taking those first uncertain steps on the moon, Aldrin, a "religious" man, asked for a moment of silence, opened a small kit prepared by his Presbyterian pastor, and poured in some wine from a tiny vial into a tiny chalice. Before going back on the air, he ate a tiny piece of bread, swallowed the wine and silently gave thanks for the intelligence and spirit that had brought two young pilots to the Sea of Tranquility.

David wrote, "When I consider your heavens . . . the moon and the stars . . . what is man . . . ?" (Ps. 8:3-4).

⇛ Giving Electronically   *December 16*

Many church members are paying their tithes electronically. Bypassing the offering plates at the church service, they have their offerings automatically deducted from their bank accounts. Churchgoers find doing it that way easier than fumbling with the traditional envelopes. It also keeps them current with pledges when away. Members enroll by filling out a form stating the gift amount, bank account number, and withdrawal day.

The automatic system overcomes the summer slump when donations often fall off. Electronic giving also is useful on bad-weather Sundays when not only are people missing but their offering envelopes are too.

Thanks!

Lutheran Brotherhood has put together an electronic funds transfer program called "Simply Giving." Whether we give by cash, check, legacy, annuity, stock or electronic transfer, if we're thankful to the Lord, our gifts will be divinely approved.

⫸ *December 17*   *A Needed Word of Encouragement*

My wife, Bernice, relates an amazing story of how God encouraged her:

"Sitting by myself one afternoon in the waiting room of a suburban Chicago hospital where I had traveled to visit my father, I felt depressed at the thought of him having to make another transition. The doctor had told my mother that he could leave the hospital but that she could not take care of him until he was able to walk. A search of nearby nursing facilities had begun. Most looked like gold-gilded birdcages to me.

"On the table was reading matter. I picked up a leaflet called *Power*, and glanced through it. I spotted the title of an article, "Discouragement is the Tool of the Devil." That sounded familiar, I thought, and looked at the author's name. It was my husband, Leslie B. Flynn. Here I was 900 miles away from home and God sent me a message of hope. I read the article, then took it in to my father and read it to him. He told me how thankful he was that I had found it. We both were thankful for we both needed this timely word of encouragement."

⫸ *December 18*   *Commanding His Angels*

Five young missionaries were speared to death beside a little jungle river in Ecuador about fifty years ago. Some years later a striking detail of the story was related by several of the killers themselves.

Right after the killings, each one saw figures moving in bright light above the trees, and they heard voices singing. They were scared because they knew it was something supernatural.

Author Thea B. Van Halsema wonders about this phenomenon:

Was it a heavenly choir to welcome the martyrs home?
Was it an incident to prepare the Huaorani for the gospel?
Was it a flash of insight into a spiritual kingdom?
Was it a glimpse of a power that could replace the terrors
  of evil spirits and the common practice of killings
  with spears?
Was it a confirmation to the families of the martyrs, and
  to us of the power of God to bring victory out of
  seemingly tragic deaths?

Hasn't the Psalmist said, "He will command his angels concerning you to guard you in all your ways" (91:11). Thank God for angels!

⇛ *His First Bible* 　　　　　　　*December 19*

When a mission director arrived in a small town in the interior of Europe, an old man stopped him in front of the church door, pulled out a faded piece of paper from his inside pocket and asked, "Mister, can you tell me what book this page came from?" The director recognized it immediately. "This is a page from the Bible, sir."

The old man looked at it fondly, then replied, "I have read this page over and over for many years. I didn't know where it came from, but I knew in my heart there was something different about these words." The director had the pleasure of giving this man a Bible, the first one he had ever seen.

In earlier centuries copies of the Bible were rare, unwieldy, in Latin, and costly. How little we realize the privilege of holding God's Word compactly in our hand or pocket. And readable in our own language. And so inexpensive the poorest family may own a copy. And it can be opened at any time without breaking the law. And printed in profusion, enough for everyone to own several copies.

Thank you, O Lord, for the freedom to read your Word!

Astronaut Frank Borman predicted, "The more we learn about the wonders of our universe, the more clearly are we going to perceive the hand of God."

Another U.S. astronaut, Guy Gardner, who flew the second shuttle after the Challenger tragedy, viewed the earth as a miniature globe compared to the vastness of God's creation—"a swirling silver-blue jewel set against an unimaginable infinity of stars." We don't have to fly in a space shuttle to appreciate the splendor of divine handiwork in a sunset, rainbow, or a radiant spectrum of changing fall colors.

Like the Psalmist we advance beyond gratitude to adoration for God's magnificence displayed in creation: "O Lord, our Lord, how majestic is your name in all the earth!" (8:9). Gratitude says, "Thank you, Lord, for giving me this gift." Adoration wonders, "How great You must be!" And those who know Him as Creator-Redeemer experience even greater joy.

Joseph and Mary, returning from Jerusalem to Nazareth after the Passover Feast, thought their 12-year-old son was in the festive crowd. At day's end they sought Jesus but found Him not. Hurrying back, they thankfully and joyfully located Him conversing in the Temple with the learned doctors.

At Yuletide Christmas carols repeatedly blare out, "Christ the Savior is born," and fall on dull ears. Many merely mouth words void of personal commitment to the incarnate Son of God as they sing, "Fall at His feet." On Good Friday thousands come to the Lord's Supper, but some fail to realize that "He was wounded for our transgressions." On Easter churches are crowded with people sporting new clothes, celebrating bunnies and eggs, but with minimum heartfelt appreciation of the empty tomb. Intellectual knowledge of Jesus Christ is meaningless unless accompanied by thankful, life-changing faith.

Just as Joseph and Mary rejoiced with thankfulness when they found the boy Jesus, so will we rejoice with gratitude and joy unspeakable when we realize His presence in our lives.

≫ *Spare Envelopes*   *December 22*

If we recognized our many occasions for thanking, we would certainly reduce our excuses for grumbling. A man bought Christmas cards and envelopes from a local printer. Several envelopes were spoiled while he was addressing them, so he had to throw away an equal number of cards. An idea struck him. The printer should include extra envelopes with each box of cards. The spare envelopes would create good will.

Enthusiastically he passed the idea on to the printer, who replied, "Oh, I thought of that years ago. I packed two extra envelopes in each box of 50 cards, but I soon stopped."

"Why? Didn't the customers appreciate the extra envelopes?"

"No, it wasn't that. Many complained their boxes were short two cards!"

A positive approach would have led to counting the cards and thanking the printer for his generous foresight.

≫ *Goodbye to a Son*   *December 23*

A leader in Wycliffe Bible Translators tells how difficult it was to leave for the mission field the first time. Bernie and Nancy May were to report to an isolated center in southern Mexico on December 28. To arrive there from Bernie's parents' home in Pennsylvania they had to leave on Christmas Day. Says Bernie, "We got up early that morning to open gifts. Mom baked a turkey for noon dinner. Everyone knew that after we ate, we'd be leaving.

"I still remember the tears in my mom's eyes as she hugged me goodbye, my father's firm handclasp, his arm around my shoulder, his 'I'm proud of you, Son.' It was hard for my father to say goodbye." How difficult for his parents to let him go, yet how inwardly thankful they were.

Yet that's what Christmas is all about, isn't it? Wasn't it on Christmas that God sent his Son? It was hard for Bernie's dad to send him; how difficult it must have been for God to send His Son to be born in a stable, knowing that in a few short years He would be crucified. Yet the Scriptures tells us why He did so: "For God so loved the world . . ." (Jn. 3:16)

❧ December 24   *A Christmas Memory*

The late James Montgomery Boice, pastor for many years of Tenth Presbyterian Church in Philadelphia, Pennsylvania, related a Christmas memory. His father had been released from World War II military service in Louisiana, and immediately headed for McKeesport, Pennsylvania, hoping to arrive by Christmas Eve. His aunt and grandmother had everything ready for a very joyful Christmas.

Late Christmas Eve, due to a snowstorm, his parents realized they would never make their destination so checked into a modest village motel. He and two sisters were disappointed. Could Santa Claus find them? Hopeful, they hung up their stockings.

Next morning they awoke to find their stockings filled with LifeSavers, gum, and candy. Says Boice, "I realized later that my parents, exhausted, must have gone out late that night, in bad weather to get what they could to meet our childish expectations. This is a happy memory for me." The three children were thrilled and thankful.

❧ December 25   *O Come Let Us Adore Him!*

A Christmas card imagined a pastor falling asleep in his study on Christmas morning and dreaming of a world to which Jesus had not come. In his dream, there were no Christmas decorations. No church spires.

A knock brought a request to come to a dying mother. At her

bedside he looked for a familiar verse to comfort her, but the Bible ended at Malachi. No Gospels, no empty tomb, no promise of life beyond the grave. At the graveside he had no message of a glorious resurrection, only "dust to dust," and one long, last, final farewell.

Suddenly, nearby music woke him with a start. He burst into praise when he realized it was his choir next door practicing:

"O, come all ye faithful, Joyful and triumphant . . .

O come let us adore Him, Christ the Lord."

Had Christ not come we would have no New Testament, no gospel, no Church, no Lord's Day, no forgiveness, no hope of glorified bodies. No wonder elderly Anna, coming up to Mary and Joseph in the temple, "gave thanks to God and spoke about the child to all" (Luke 2:38).

⋙ *When Thanklessness Is Unthinkable* *December 26*

Medical missionary Dr. Fred Scovel, his wife Myra, and their five children were repatriated from a Japanese concentration camp when World War II broke out. At first, food was difficult to eat. Their prison fare had often been rice with worms. Myra Scovel, weak and pregnant, wondered if they would reach New York before her baby was born.

When they boarded the Swedish ship Gripsholm, a smorgasbord awaited them. How thankful the Scovels were, but how little they could eat. Their stomachs had shrunk.

The Scovels were the first off the boat in New York. The ambulance raced through the city to Presbyterian Hospital where their baby was born just yards from the delivery room. Headlines read, "Race With Stork Episode."

The morning after arrival the children were eating breakfast in the hotel coffee shop. A stranger, finding no vacant table, joined them. When his order arrived, he called the waitress to complain about the eggs. One of the boys pushed the plate back in front of him, saying, "Eat it. It's food." To the boys ingratitude was inexcusable.

We owe the Jew the knowledge of the one true God. Without them we would be bowing down to gods of wood and stone.

We owe the Jew the Bible, the world's best seller that has been translated into more languages than any other book.

We owe the Jew our code of values. The source of our morality has been traced to the Ten Commandments.

We owe the Church to the Jew. The first church was a Jewish church, beginning in Jewish Jerusalem. For the first few years every member was a Jew. When we think of a church today, we think of a sanctuary full of Gentiles. Back then it was just the reverse—exclusively Jewish—no Gentiles.

We owe the Messiah to the Jews. Events in the life of Jesus fulfilled Old Testament prophecies. Probably no chapter speaks more clearly of the sufferings and victory of the Messiah than Isaiah 53. To the Jews we owe a huge debt of gratitude.

❧ *December 28*   **A Prayer of Thanks for Everything**

(From the private prayers of Bishop Lancelot Andrews, a principal translator of the King James Version Bible):

"O LORD, MY LORD, for my being, life, reason, for nurture, protection, guidance, for education, civil rights, for Thy gifts of nature, grace, fortune, for redemption, regeneration, catechizing, for my call, recall, yea, many calls besides; for Thy long long-suffering, toward me, many seasons, many years, up to this time;

"For all good things received, successes granted me, good things done; for the use of things present, for Thy promise and my hope of the enjoyment of good things to come; for my parents honest and good, teachers kind, benefactors never to be forgotten, religious intimates congenial, hearers thoughtful, friends sincere, domestics faithful;

"For all who have advantaged me, by writings, homilies, converse, prayers, patterns, rebukes, injuries; for all these, open, hidden, remembered, forgotten; I confess to Thee and will confess, I bless Thee and will bless, I give thanks to Thee and will give thanks, all the days of my life."

⇒ *Thanksgivings in Heaven*   *December 29*

The 24 elders in heaven, probably representing the redeemed of all ages, express their appreciation for their salvation, singing a new song: "You are worthy to take the scroll and to open its seals, because you were slain, and with your blood you purchased men for God from every tribe and language and people and nation" (Rev. 5:9).

Later we read that the 24 elders fall on their faces saying, "We give thanks to you, Lord God Almighty, the One who is, and who was, because you have taken your great power and have begun to reign" (Rev. 11:16-17).

"Hallelujah," a glowing word of adoration, does not appear in the Bible till near the end of the New Testament where it resounds from the sky as the voice of a countless crowd, shouting "Hallelujah! Salvation and glory and power belong to our God" (Rev. 19:1). Three times in the next five verses sweet voices speak out this paean of indescribable delight.

In heaven prayer may cease, but thanksgiving will remain.

⇒ *A Brother's Love*   *December 30*

In 1972 Gary Cobb was a rebellious teenager into drugs. His brother, Terry, became a Christian and began to tell him of Jesus.

A few days after Christmas, Terry, at work in a supermarket, was shot by two robbers and left paralyzed. Says Gary, "I thought about what Terry told me about Jesus. On New Year's Day 1973, in the hospital prayer room, I asked the Lord for forgiveness. I told Terry of my decision to give my life to Christ. Terry couldn't speak but he smiled with joy. A few days later he died.

"Six months later I was working in the same supermarket.

Thanks!

One day when I was telling a stock-boy about Jesus, he said, 'Your brother used to tell me the same thing. I told him that he ought to talk to you—that you needed Christ more than anyone I knew.'

"I asked, 'What did Terry say to that?' The stock-boy replied, 'Your brother said that he would give his life if you could come to know the Lord Jesus.'"

Said Gary, "Terry's concern for me was what led me to Christ. He was willing to die for me. I'm so thankful for his love."

➢ *December 31*   *New Year's Eve Celebration*

One New Year's Eve a group of drinkers were celebrating in a noisy hotel barroom. Also present was Sam, the local pastor's wayward son. The town's hardened skeptic walked in. "They're having a Watch Night service over in the church. I don't see why we can't have one here." Mocking a ministerial tone, the skeptic asked another celebrant, "Brother Eldridge, please lead in prayer." He gave a mock prayer.

After a raucous hymn, he said, "Brother Sam will now preach the sermon." Sam objected but was overruled. Cornered, he began mumbling about repenting of old sinful ways and starting a new life. He began to sound sincere as fragments of his deceased mother's prayers came to mind. Bible verses from Sunday school and truths his father had preached all came tumbling out with new force. His audience, at first resentful, became silent. Sam was soon down on his knees on the barroom floor, asking the Lord to forgive him. Two other men were converted that night.

As Sam headed home, he overtook his aged father, feebly making his way home from his Watch Night service. What joy when Sam told him what happened. His father stayed up the rest of the night, thanking God over and over.

CREDITS

January 1: St. Paul's *Printer,* Society of St. Paul, from *The Anglican Digest,* Advent 2001, p. 40.

January 2: Sevig, Julie B., "Refugee Says Thanks." Reprinted by permission from *The Lutheran,* December 2000, p. 37. Copyright © 2000 Augsburg Fortress.

January 4: "The Lord in Black Skin," *Christianity Today,* October 2, 2000. Used by permission of the Rev. Dr. Pamela Baker Powell.

January 6: Hansen, Christine, "God's Quizzical Ways," *The Lutheran,* August 2000, p. 31. Copyright © 2000 Augsburg Fortress. Adapted by permission.

January 13: Beers, V. Gilbert, "Two Nobodies," Wheaton College *Alumni,* Summer 1999, p. 48. Copyright © V. Gilbert Beers. Used by permission.

January 15: Adapted from Hayford, Jack W., *Worship His Majesty,* Ventura, CA: Gospel Light/Regal Books. Copyright © 1981. Used by permission.

January 23: Keiper, Ralph L., *The Power of Biblical Thinking,* Old Tappan, NJ: Fleming H. Revell Co., 1979, pp. 35-37.

January 24: Ibid., pp. 37-38.

January 25: Haegeland, Kari, "No 'Wright' Choice for Chaplain of Congress," in The King's College *Vision,* Vol. 3, Issue 2, Summer 2000. Used by permission.

January 26: Smith, Rev. Brad, *Souper Good News,* p. 2, Souper Bowl Inc., 125 Sparkleberry Lane, Columbia, SC, 29229.

January 28: Pippert, Wesley G., "New Doctor for the U.S.," *Christian Life,* May 1982, pp. 32-36. Used by permission.

January 29: Flynn, Leslie B., *Did I Say Thanks?,* Nashville: Broadman Press, 1963, pp. 112-113.
Note: Many items in *Did I Say Thanks?* appear in various devotionals in this book.

February 1: News Summary, September 9, 2000, http://religiontoday.crosswalk.com.

Thanks!

February 7: Morris, Harold, with Barker, Dianne, *Twice Pardoned,* Nantucket Publishing, pp. 60-62. Used by permission of Edwin Tucker Publishing, Wilson, NC, 27893.

February 9: Dobson, Dr. James C., "The Most Influential Person of the Past 1000 Years," Dr. James Dobson's *Family News,* December 1999.

February 16: Yancey, Philip, *Reaching for the Invisible God,* Grand Rapids: Zondervan, 2000, p. 118ff. Used by permission.

February 17: Greene, Bob, "Sincerely, John Kennedy," *Chicago Tribune,* July 28, 1999. Copyright © Tribune Media Services, Chicago, IL, 60611. All rights reserved. Reprinted with permission.

February 21: Buchanan, Mark, "Trapped in the Cult of the Next Thing," *Christianity Today,* September 6, 1999, pp. 63-72. Used by permission.

February 23: Packer, James I., *Rediscovering Holiness,* Ann Arbor, MI: Servant Publications, 1992, p. 75.

February 29: Petrescue, Dave, "Signs," *Alliance Life,* back cover, October 2004.

March 5: Lambeth Report, "Knock, Knock," from *The Anglican Digest,* Whitsuntide A.D. 2000, p. 12. Used by permission.

April 3: Trammel, Madison, "A Day to Remember," *In Other Words,* Fall 2000, p. 22. Published by Wycliffe Bible Translators. Used by permission.

April 5: Register, John F., "My Time of Trusting," *Decision,* July-August 2000. Copyright © 2000 by Billy Graham Evangelistic Association. All rights reserved. Used by permission.

April 18: From "Jan's Journal," *Missionary Monthly,* August-September 2000, p. 21. Used by permission.

April 19: Ibid., p. 22.

April 26: Beckman, Allan, *The Niihav Incident,* Honolulu: Heritage Press of the Pacific, pp. 107-108.

May 5: Montgomery, Elsie, "What We Need, When We Need It," *Decision,* July-August 2000. Copyright © 2000 by Billy Graham Evangelistic Association. All rights reserved. Used by permission.

May 6: Cavanaugh, Rev. Brian: "Unthanked People," *The Joyful Newsletter,* November 1999. Published by the Fellowship of Merry Christians, Portage, Michigan.

May 16: News Summary, August 9, 2000, http://religiontoday.crosswalk.com.

May 24: Parachin, Victor, "God's 911," *Christian Reader,* September/October 2000, p. 65ff. Used by permission.

May 27: Canberg, Mary, "Rockland County Youth String Orchestra," *America String Teacher,* Spring 1979, pp. 16-17.

June 10: Smith, Alfred B., *Al Smith's Treasury of Hymn Stories,* Montrose, PA: Heritage Music, Inc., 1982, pp. 267-269.

June 11: Glaser, Mitch, "An Attitude of Gratitude," *The Chosen People,* November 2000, pp. 2-3.

June 12: Yancey, Philip, *What's So Amazing About Grace?,* Grand Rapids: Zondervan, 1977, p. 190. Used by permission.

June 13: Yancey, Philip, "My To-Be List: What I Learned from a 50-Year Spiritual Check-Up," *Christianity Today,* April 3, 2000. Used by permission.

June 19: Zornes, Jeanne, "The Barnabas Committee— Encouraging One Another," *Decision,* December 2000. Copyright © 2000 by Billy Graham Evangelistic Association. All rights reserved. Used by permission.

June 22: Boyd, Leslie, "Won't You Please, Please Say Thank You?", *The Journal News,* West Nyack, NY, C1, November 6, 1993.

June 25: Marks, Marsha, "Special Delivery," *Christian Reader,* September/October 2000, pp. 15-17. Used by permission. Marsha Marks is the author of *101 Amazing Things About God,* Riveroak Publishing. This story appears in a longer version in that book.

June 27: Bishop, Gary L., President of Missionary Aviation Fellowship, in "A Mother's Day Letter to Constituents," dated April 25, 2000. Used by permission.

July 4: Dr. James Dobson's Focus on the Family *Bulletin,* Aug. 1, 2000.

July 8: "A 20th Century Missionary Autobiography—Part 23,"

translated by Rev. Chan Thleng, *Missionary Monthly,* August-September 2000, p. 27. Used by permission.

July 18: Briner, Bob, "Saying Thanks: A Simple Way to Disciple Communities," *Pen and Sword,* November/December 2000. Published by Amy Foundation. Used by permission.

July 21: Brickner, David, "Thanksgiving Is a Three-Way Street," *Jews for Jesus* newsletter, November 1999.

July 26: "Letters to the Editor," in the Princeton Theological Seminary alumni magazine *inSpire,* Spring 2000, pp. 2-3.

July 29: Trexler, Edgar R., "Judgment and Grace at Nuremberg," *The Lutheran,* March 1999. Copyright © 1999 Augsburg Fortress. Reprinted by permission.

August 2: Thurston, Lucy G., "ARTICLE X—A Surgical Operation," *The Life and Times of Lucy G. Thurston, Pioneer Missionary to the Sandwich Islands,* 2nd edition, Ann Arbor: S.C. Andrews, 1921, pp. 168-176.

August 4: Kaminski, Marek, "My Left-Handed Bible," *Christianity Today,* October 23, 1995, p. 24.

August 8: Lewis, C.S., *The Quotable Lewis,* Tyndale House Publishers, 1989, p. 579.

August 10: Wade, Mildred Renfro, "My Words: What I'd Like to Do," *Arthritis Today,* November-December 2000, p. 6. This is part of a longer piece, "I'd Like To . . ." by the author. Used by permission.

August 15: Cheatham, M.D., Mel, "He Took My Place," *Decision,* April 2001. Copyright © 2001 Billy Graham Evangelistic Association. All rights reserved. Used by permission.

August 18: Smith, Alfred B., *Al Smith's Treasury of Hymn Stories,* pp. 249-251.

September 2: Ibid.

September 3: Tract, "Seven Men Went Singing Into Heaven," Good News Publishing Co. Originally translated by Clara Becker for the Salvation Army *War Cry* magazine.

September 6: Hastings, Jennifer, "Life Goes On," *Decision,* September 2000. Copyright © 2000 Billy Graham Evangelistic

Association. All rights reserved. Used by permission.

September 10: Carey, George, Archbishop of Canterbury, "The Archbishop's Voice," from *The Anglican Digest*, Transfiguration 2000, p. 63. Used by permission.

September 19: Bruning, Carol L., "Pocketful of Prayers," *Decision*, September 1994. Copyright © 1994 Billy Graham Evangelistic Association. All rights reserved. Used by permission.

September 24: "Canja Praises Young Teller Who Aided Scam Victim," in AARP Bulletin, September 2000, p. 13.

October 3: O'Connor, Karen, "The Blessing Bag," *Christian Reader*, November/December 2000, pp. 41-42. Used by permission.

October 7: "Fighting Leprosy at 8,500 Feet," *Flight Watch*, MAF Worldwide Ministry News, Vol. 15, No. 4, July 2000. Used by permission.

October 9: Jennings, Muriel Van Orden" (first woman graduate of Princeton Theological Seminary), "A Clothes Call," *inSpire*, Summer/Fall 2000. Used by permission.

October 11: Current Feature Story, August 3, 2000, http://religiontoday.crosswalk.com.

October 17: Widenhouse, Kathy, "Be a Barnabas to Your Pastor," *Focus on the Family*, September 2000. Used by permission.

October 22: Rosen, Moishe, "The Name of Jesus," *Jews for Jesus* newsletter, September 2000.

October 23: Smith, Alfred B., *Al Smith's Treasury of Hymn Stories*, pp. 268-269.

October 24: Lacey, Robert, and Danziger, Danny, *The Year 1000*, New York: Little Brown & Co., 1999, pp. 119, 136, and 194.

October 25: Ibid.

November 2: Curtis, Barbara, "Grateful for What I Never Had," *The Plain Truth*, November/December 1999. Used by permission.

November 10: "A Millennium Story," *South of the Mountain*, 2000, Rockland County Historical Society, pp. 19-20. Used by permission.

November 23: Retton, Mary Lou, with Bender, David, *Gateways to Happiness,* New York: Broadway Books, 2000, p. 66. Used by permission.

November 25: Curtis, Barbara, "Thanksgiving: The Whole Story," *Focus on the Family,* November 2000, pp. 21-22. Used by permission.

November 27: Hall, Rev. Dwight in *Alliance Life,* April 2002, p. 27.

December 5: Britton, Joan S. "Oh . . . It's Corrie ten Boom!" *TWR Magazine* (Trans World Radio), December 1982. Used by permission.

December 8: Retton, Mary Lou, with Bender, David, *Gateways to Happiness,* p. 39. Used by permission.

December 12: Steffen, Bonnie, "Living Letters," *Christian Reader,* November/December, pp. 18-26. Used by permission.

December 14: Lovegren, Rev. Levi A., *"True Appreciation,"* in a church bulletin.

December 16: News Summary, November 21, 2000, http://religiontoday.crosswalk.com.

December 18: Van Halsema, Thea B., "Bright Light Above the Trees," *Missionary Monthly,* November, 1996, p. 3. Used by permission.

December 23: May, Bernie, "Christmas: A Day for Leaving," in Wycliffe's *Focus,* December/1997/January 1998. Used by permission.

December 28: Andrews, Bishop Lancelot, "Abundant Thanks," from *The Anglican Digest,* Michaelmas 1997, p. 46. Used by permission.

December 30: Cobb, Gary, "My Brother's Love," *Decision,* October 2000. Copyright © 2000 Billy Graham Evangelistic Association. All rights reserved. Used by permission.

Other great books by Leslie B. Flynn!

What the Church Owes the Jew
~Leslie B. Flynn

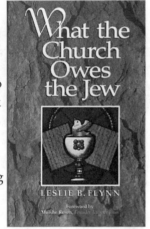

What do you know about the unique Jewish contribution to the Scriptures, the Church, and to the world at-large?
Dr. Leslie Flynn, who served as pastor to many Jewish Christians in the New York area, passionately shares these answers and more (e.g., anti-Semitism, the Jewishness of Jesus), to help Jews and non-Jews build bridges of understanding and friendship.
ISBN 0-9654806-3-1 paper $12.00

Jesus in the Image of God:
A Challenge to Christlikeness
~Leslie B. Flynn

A great book for Bible study groups!
Here's a real antidote to the negative and faithless views of the Jesus Seminar. Let the Jesus of the Gospels challenge you to become more like him—the Son of God created in God's own image, who overcame despair, sorrow, rejection, and humiliation to bring healing, redemption, hope, and the Good News of God's love to all human beings.
ISBN 0-9654806-1-5 paper $12.00

$\mathcal{G}$REAT BOOKS TO ENRICH YOUR LIFE!

The Lord's Prayer for a New Millennium
~Isabel Anders

What if an exploration of every aspect of the mysteries of life revealed an intricate design in praise of an intelligent Creator?
Your knowledge of God and the world you live in will soar to new levels as you explore the theme of God and science in the devotional setting of the Lord's Prayer. Stunning new insights of God will captivate you through glimpses of a scientific correlation with God's creation.
ISBN 0-9654806-8-2 paper $12.95

Canine Parables: *Portraits of God and Life*
~Paulette Zubel

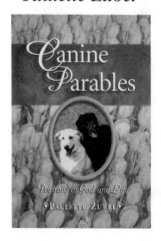

Can God's creatures teach us about him?
Paulette Zubel emphatically says, "Yes!" By observing her dogs' wacky and winsome antics, she reflects, through 63 devotionals, God's loving nature and our relationship with him. The old saying, "a dog is man's best friend," gets a new twist in *Canine Parables.* Paulette's dogs remind us that *God* is our best friend.
ISBN 0-9654806-4-X paper $12.95